When Christians First
Met Muslims

When Christians First Met Muslims

A Sourcebook of the Earliest Syriac Writings on Islam

Michael Philip Penn

UNIVERSITY OF CALIFORNIA PRESS

University of California Press, one of the most distinguished university presses in the United States, enriches lives around the world by advancing scholarship in the humanities, social sciences, and natural sciences. Its activities are supported by the UC Press Foundation and by philanthropic contributions from individuals and institutions. For more information, visit www.ucpress.edu.

University of California Press
Oakland, California

© 2015 by The Regents of the University of California

Library of Congress Cataloging-in-Publication Data

Penn, Michael Philip, author.
    When Christians first met Muslims : a sourcebook of the earliest Syriac writings on Islam / Michael Philip Penn.
        p.   cm.
    Includes bibliographical references and index..
    ISBN 978-0-520-28493-7 (cloth, alk. paper) —
    ISBN 978-0-520-28494-4 (pbk., alk. paper) —
    ISBN 978-0-520-96057-2 (electronic)
    1. Islam—Early works to 1800.   2. Christianity and other religions—Islam—History—To 1500—Sources.   3. Islam—Relations—Christianity—History—To 1500—Sources.   4. Syriac Christians—History—To 1500—Sources.   I. Title.
BP160.P46   2015
261.2′709021—dc23   2014034643

Manufactured in the United States of America

24   23   22   21   20   19   18   17   16   15
10   9   8   7   6   5   4   3   2   1

In keeping with a commitment to support environmentally responsible and sustainable printing practices, UC Press has printed this book on Natures Natural, a fiber that contains 30% post-consumer waste and meets the minimum requirements of ANSI/NISO Z39.48-1992 (R 1997) (*Permanence of Paper*).

For Sarah, Sasha, and Tabitha

CONTENTS

ACKNOWLEDGMENTS

This book was made possible by four institutions. It never would have come into being were it not for the incredible generosity of an American Council for Learned Societies Frederick Burkhardt Residential Fellowship, which funded a year of research leave. That year was spent at the National Humanities Center, whose hospitality and truly amazing staff have given it the well deserved reputation of being "academic heaven." The first pages of the project, however, began under the auspices of New York University's Institute for the Study of the Ancient World, which also generously supported my work. And through it all, Mount Holyoke College not only allowed me to take advantage of these opportunities but also provided additional support, especially in the form of travel and research assistant grants, that allowed this all to come together.

I also have been sustained by an incredible network of friends, colleagues, and mentors. Gabriel Aydin, Uriel Simonsohn, and Lucas Van Rompay kindly looked through various parts of my translations. Rhonda Burnette-Bletsch, Suleiman Mourad, and

Michael Pregill provided valuable revisions for the introduction. The entire book was made better through the suggestions of two anonymous readers for University of California Press. The writing itself was vastly improved through the editorial assistance of Juliana Froggatt; Laura Poole, the founder of Archer Editorial Services; and Cindy Fulton at UC Press. I am still overwhelmed by the enthusiasm my editor Eric Schmidt has had for this project and for his expertise and kindness throughout the publication process. But most important has been the emotional support I have constantly received from my family, from a wonderful group of best friends, and from my *Doktormutter,* Liz Clark.

PROLOGUE

THE YEAR 630

The year is 630 according to the Christian calendar, and the Byzantine emperor Heraclius is celebrating at the center of the world. Through a daring sneak attack that still impresses military historians, he has just defeated the Sasanian King of Kings, concluding a twenty-five-year war between the Byzantine and Persian Empires. To crown his victory, Heraclius triumphantly processes into Jerusalem, to the Church of the Resurrection, the "navel of the world," where Adam was thought to be buried and Christ resurrected. Sixteen years earlier the Persians had wrested Jerusalem from Byzantine control, gained possession of this church, and captured Jesus's true cross. In 630 Heraclius is reversing all of this. As part of their peace settlement with the Byzantines, the Persians have returned Jesus's cross to Heraclius, and this relic now leads his exultant procession into the recently reclaimed holy city and holy sepulcher. It is hard to think of a more appropriate or a more carefully staged ending to a war that many have labeled the first true crusade.

In 630 Heraclius has a lot to celebrate. Twenty years earlier, this son of a Byzantine general rebelled against Emperor Phocas (d. 610), who in turn had come to power through the murder of his predecessor, Emperor Maurice (d. 602). As the last one standing after a series of coups, Heraclius took charge of an empire fraught with military and theological challenges. His most immediate concern was the ongoing campaigns against the Persians. In 602 the Sasanian king had used Phocas's murder of Maurice as a pretext to invade Byzantine territory. Heraclius's murder of Phocas did not end Persian advances, which simply intensified. In 614 the Persians gained control of Jerusalem and the true cross. It took Heraclius ten years to begin turning the tide. In 624 he headed a military campaign into Armenia that eventually brought him through Mesopotamia and, in 628, to the outskirts of the Persian capital of Ctestiphon, twenty miles from modern-day Baghdad. His military successes prompted a Persian coup and subsequent capitulation.

Now, in 630, the return of the cross seals a quarter century of warfare. But though Heraclius's entry through Jerusalem's Golden Gate symbolizes a militarily united Byzantium, it does not lessen the vast theological rifts that continue to divide his empire. His rule inherited centuries of intra-Christian strife. By all accounts, he soon made the situation even worse. At stake were the increasingly heated debates regarding Christology: how best to describe the relationship between Christ's divinity and Christ's humanity.

Two hundred years earlier, these controversies had surfaced when Constantinople's Bishop Nestorius declared that Jesus's mother should not be called "the bearer of God." Nestorius and his supporters argued that Mary could not have given birth to Christ's divine nature, only to his human nature. From their perspective, only by keeping Christ's human nature and his divine nature conceptually separate could one avoid the blasphemous belief that during the Crucifixion God himself had suffered and died. In 431 Nestorius was outmaneuvered by his nemesis Cyril of Alexander, and the Council of Ephesus ruled that Nestorius and the views attributed to him were heretical. For Nestorius, this meant exile. For Christianity, this meant a division that continues to this day.

By the fifth century there were already many Christians for whom some version of the two-nature Christology espoused by Nestorius and his teacher Theodore of Mopsuestia was a central theological dogma. This was particularly the case for the Church of the East, primarily located in Persian territory. By anathemizing these beliefs, the Council of Ephesus further separated the Church of the East from the rest of Christianity. This church continues today. Present-day adherents are often called Assyrian Christians or, more disparagingly, Nestorians. Twenty-first-century scholars more often refer to members of the Church of the East as East Syrians.

In 451 the Byzantine emperor Marcian convened the even more divisive Council of Chalcedon. The council's decision that Christ was "in two natures" became official doctrine for the Byzantine Church and eventually for Roman Catholicism and Protestantism. Many, however, saw the council as artificially dividing Christ into two parts and undermining the central importance of his incarnation as the key to salvation. During the fifth, sixth, and seventh centuries, opponents of the council's decision began to consolidate into several anti-Chalcedonian churches, such as the Armenian, Coptic, and Ethiopic Churches. In the geographic area most central to this book, the predominant anti-Chalcedonian church is what modern scholars call the

West Syrian or the Syrian Miaphysite Church. This church also continues today, and in the twenty-first century its official name is now the Syrian Orthodox Church. Its Miaphysite adherents are disparagingly called Monophysites or Jacobites.

By 630 Heraclius has already spent two decades dealing with this array of churches. The Byzantine church that he supports is Chalcedonian. Yet many Christians living in Byzantine territory are Syrian Miaphysites (also known as West Syrians, Syrian Orthodox, Jacobites, or Monophysites) or, in some cases, East Syrians (also called members of the Church of the East, Assyrian Christians, or Nestorians). A linguistic divide further cements these divisions, as most Syrian Miaphysites and East Syrian Christians speak and write not Greek but the lingua franca of the late ancient Middle East, the Aramaic dialect of Syriac.

Soon Heraclius will make this situation even more complicated. The emperor will try to circumvent the juggernaut of discussing Christ's nature by instead speaking of Christ as having a single will. Heraclius's attempts to forcefully impose this Monothelete doctrine even on fellow Chalcedonians will lead to the creation of yet another church, the Maronites. As a result, even though the Christians examined in this book belonged to a single linguistic community—they all spoke Syriac—they comprised four competing confessional communities: East Syrians, Miaphysites, Chalcedonians, and Maronites.

Heraclius is trying to overshadow these theological divisions with his triumphal entry into Jerusalem. But no amount of pomp and circumstance can eclipse his ongoing persecution of non-Chalcedonian Christians. It turns out, however, that the greatest threat to his empire will come not from recently defeated Persians or from dissenting Christians but from a group that up until this point he has mainly ignored.

In 630 Heraclius is not the only late ancient military leader to process into a sacred city. In the same year, 750 miles to the southeast, the prophet Muḥammad triumphantly returns to Mecca. According to Muslim tradition, he first began receiving divine revelations the same year that Heraclius came into power. Then, while Heraclius was engaged in his campaigns against the Persians, Muḥammad was fighting his own battles. First he struggled to form a fledgling community of believers in his hometown of Mecca. Next, in 622 he relocated that community two hundred miles to the north, to the city of Yathrib, later named Medina, a migration (hijra) so important in Muslim tradition that all later years are dated relative to the hijra (A.H.). Finally, while Heraclius was campaigning through Armenia and Mesopotamia, in Arabia Muḥammad led the Medinans on a series of military ventures against the Meccans, whom he defeated in 630 when he took control of Mecca and its sacred shrine, the Kaʿba.

In 630 it is unlikely that Heraclius has heard much about Muḥammad. As part of their ongoing conflict with each other, the Byzantine and Persian Empires had frequently bribed various Arab tribes or employed them as mercenaries. But neither Heraclius nor his Persian contemporaries ever imagined that the tribes of Arabia could effectively unite around a single figure. So Muḥammad's death in 632 will pass unremarked by the Byzantines and the Persians. Both empires will also mainly ignore Muḥammad's successor, Abū Bakr, as he consolidates the Arab tribes in the *ridda* wars of 632–33.

In early 634 Heraclius will most likely be in Damascus when he hears about the Arab defeat of a Byzantine garrison near Gaza. Soon afterward he will receive reports of major Syrian cities falling under Arab control. In response, he will send in substantial Byzantine troops. The Arabs will defeat the majority of these, most resoundingly in 636 at the Battle of Yarmuk, after which Arab forces will take effective control of all of Syria as Heraclius makes a strategic withdrawal. The Persians will face a similar phenomenon, with the first military engagements occurring in 634 and a fairly continuous loss of territory continuing throughout the late 630s and early 640s. Unlike the Byzantines, they will eventually lose their entire empire, with the last Sasanian king dying in 651.

In the 630s and 640s, the physical destruction and human casualties from the Islamic conquests will be substantially less devastating than those of the Byzantine-Persian wars that preceded them. With a few notable exceptions, the majority of sustained military engagements will take place in the countryside, minimizing civilian casualties, and most cities will capitulate to Arab forces without prolonged siege. The conquests will not leave the type of destruction layers associated with much more devastating invasions. Instead, inscriptional evidence will witness continual church occupation and even new construction throughout the period. This does not mean that the Islamic conquests will be of little consequence for the indigenous populations. But it does remind us that the conquests' political and theological ramifications will have little correlation to the number of lives lost.

In 636 Heraclius will leave Syria for Constantinople. Later authors will repeatedly depict this retreat in the starkest of terms. For example, the medieval Syriac *Chronicle ad 1234* will state:

An Arab Christian came to Antioch and told Heraclius of the Roman armies' destruction and that no messenger had escaped. In great sorrow, the Emperor Heraclius left Antioch and entered Constantinople. It has been said that when he bid Syria farewell and said "*Sozou* Syria," that is "Good-bye, Syria," [Heraclius was] like someone who had given up all hope. He raised the staff held in his hand and permitted his armies to take and plunder everything they found, as if Syria already belonged to the enemy.

The Greek historiographic tradition will be more sympathetic to Heraclius but often more filled with pathos. From these writers will emerge the often repeated claim that his despair becomes so debilitating that Heraclius develops incurable hydrophobia, preventing him from ever crossing the Bosporus Strait to enter Constantinople proper.

The year 630 makes Heraclius such a melodramatic figure. He so carefully stages his entrance into Jerusalem as a triumph. But in retrospect, this scene can transform so easily into the opening act of a tragedy. Intending to mark the beginning of a new age, Heraclius chooses to enter Jerusalem on March 21, a date traditionally associated with the day that God created the sun and the moon. Four years later a new age will indeed come, but an age very different from what Heraclius and his contemporaries expect.

The year 630 is, however, also a liminal moment. Lingering over Heraclius's procession just before it enters Jerusalem provides the opportunity to gaze back and forward. Looking back to the Christological controversies and the Byzantine-Persian wars, one gains a better understanding of the context in which the competing churches of East Syrians, Miaphysites, Chalcedonians, and Maronites developed. Looking forward to the Islamic conquests, one foresees an event that will forever change these communities. As soon as the once jubilant Heraclius flees back to Constantinople, he will leave the Syriac churches to a new world empire. Under Muslim control from then on, Syriac Christians will become the first Christians to encounter the emerging religion of Islam and the first to interpret this dramatic change of fortune.

Introduction

The year 630 and those immediately following are a turning point not simply for world history but also for the modern study of world history. Until recently, most historians traveled the same route Heraclius did: as soon as they reached the time of Muḥammad's death, their studies quickly retreated westward, concentrating on either the European Middle Ages or the later Byzantine Empire. Even those historians interested in Christian-Muslim interactions quickly shifted to a more Western perspective, focusing on conflicts between the Byzantine and Islamic Empires or on relations between Islam and the Latin West.

Starting in post-Enlightenment Europe, a different type of historian began to emerge. Originally called orientalists and more recently Islamicists, these historians were often trained in Western universities but consciously went in the opposite direction than Heraclius. Focusing on the post-630s Middle East, they often specialized in the history of early Muslims.

As a result, most modern historians of late antiquity and the early Middle Ages said either good-bye to Syria and the rest of the Middle East (just as Heraclius allegedly had) or good-bye to Christianity. If one studied Christian sources written after the 630s, one almost certainly studied the writings of Western Christians, primarily in the languages of Greek and Latin. If one studied what happened in the Middle East after the 630s, one almost certainly studied the writings of early Muslims, primarily in the languages of Arabic and Persian.

Although pragmatic, this division of scholarly labor was also problematic. For those interested in the history of early Christianity, ignoring the post-630s churches in the Middle East meant ignoring almost half of that period's Christians. For those interested in the history of the early Middle East, ignoring Middle Eastern Christians meant ignoring the majority of people inhabiting that region; in the first centuries of the Islamic Empire, the population was not mainly Muslim but Christian. As long as there remained a divide between scholars of Christian sources who focused on the West and scholars of the Middle East who focused on Muslim sources, modern narratives of the later part of late antiquity and the beginning of the Middle Ages would continue to exclude most of the people alive at that time.

Two additional factors further marginalized Middle Eastern Christianity. The first was linguistic. Many Middle Eastern Christians did not use Greek or Latin, the languages most commonly studied by church historians. So too during much of the time when Christians were the majority population of the Middle East, many did not use Arabic or Persian, the languages most commonly studied by Islamicists. Because the writings they left behind were in the "wrong" languages, they rarely appeared in modern scholarship. The second factor was theological. Due to the Christological divisions that Heraclius also had struggled with, Protestants, Roman Catholics, and Greek and Russian Orthodox deem most Middle Eastern churches heterodox. Because almost all church historians, at least until recently, were closely affiliated with a tradition that considered Middle Eastern Christians to be heretics, their history was routinely excluded from serious consideration. For different but no less pervasive reasons, most Muslim scholars deemphasized the role of Middle Eastern Christians in the early Islamic Empire.

In the past decades, however, this has begun to change. With the emergence of the field of religious studies, the study of premodern Christianity has become less tied to confessional allegiances. As late antiquity has emerged as its own subfield and become defined by many as increasingly later, the seventh through ninth centuries have gained more attention among historians. With a surging interest in a "global Middle Ages," medieval studies has become much more supportive of scholarship about the Middle East. Most important, the field of Islamic studies has become one of the most rapidly expanding disciplines in the Western academy.

The recognition of how important Middle Eastern Christianity is for a proper understanding of world history has been a gradual process. Nevertheless, it was greatly accelerated by a 1977 book titled *Hagarism: The Making of the Islamic World.* Written by the Islamicists Patricia Crone and Michael Cook, *Hagarism* presents a controversial reassessment of Islamic origins based primarily on early Christian sources that previously were known to only a few specialists. Most ended up rejecting *Hagarism*'s conclusions about the formation of early Islam. But the book's main methodological point ended up winning the day. After the publication of *Hagarism,* it became axiomatic that a historian could not do serious scholarship of the early Islamic world without taking early Christian sources seriously. Nevertheless, this has not always been an easy axiom to put into practice.

Few oppose a more chronologically, geographically, and religiously inclusive approach to history. But divisions born from the traditional boundaries of academic disciplines and linguistic training often prevent this from becoming a reality. Some branches of Middle Eastern Christianity have been easier than others to incorporate into Western scholarship and teaching. For example, Middle Eastern Christians writing in Greek, such as John of Damascus, have been much more carefully studied. The dozen or so pages John wrote about Islam are frequently cited, translated, and assigned in undergraduate and graduate classes. Writings in Arabic by Christians are rarely found on course syllabi but are accessible to most Islamicists due to their linguistic training. Similarly, the extremely important seventh-century Armenian work attributed to Sebeos benefits from an excellent modern translation and is thus often cited by modern scholars, even if only a few of them can read Armenian.

The largest and most diverse collection of early Christian texts about Islam, however, was written in the Aramaic dialect of Syriac, because Syriac served as the lingua franca for much of the late ancient Middle East. These documents have fared less well. In the decades following the publication of *Hagarism,* scholars of late antiquity and the early Middle Ages have become increasingly aware of how important Syriac sources are for the study of the early Islamic period. Nevertheless, these texts' number and diversity, the very factors that make them so precious, have also inhibited their wider study.

Scholars of Syriac have produced editions and translations of most of these works. The results of their labor, however, remain scattered, mainly in hard-to-find journals and specialist publications. These became easier to navigate with the publication of Robert Hoyland's *Seeing Islam as Others Saw It* in 1997 and *Christian-Muslim Relations: A Bibliographic History*, volume 1, edited by David Thomas and Barbara Roggema, in 2009, which provided a several-page summary, an essential bibliography, and a number of short excerpts of early Christian texts on Islam, including most of the Syriac corpus. But these publications lacked what is most important for specialist and nonspecialist alike—the texts themselves. In 1993, Andrew Palmer's *The Seventh Century in the West-Syrian Chronicles* partially ameliorated the dearth of easily accessible translations. Palmer provided brief critical introductions and fresh translations of more than a dozen seventh-century Syriac works. But as his title suggests, he focused on a specific genre of Syriac literature and did not include East Syrian texts.

When Christians First Met Muslims builds on this important shift in the study of premodern history. Modeled on Palmer's volume, it puts between two covers introductions, new translations, and a bibliography for almost every known Syriac text on Islam written prior to the Abbasid revolution of 750. Even for specialists of Syriac studies, it will be convenient to have all these translations and an up-to-date bibliography in one place. For scholars of early Islam, such a compilation is much more important, as few have the time to make the dozens of interlibrary loan requests necessary to obtain translations of most of these texts into a modern language (or, in some cases, nineteenth-century Latin), not to mention keeping up with the scholarship on these sources. *When Christians First Met Muslims* is also designed for nonspecialists, whether they be scholars of another place or time period, graduate or undergraduate students, or more general readers, because the import of these texts extends far beyond the boundary of any single academic discipline.

IMAGES OF ISLAM

This book's collection of twenty-eight texts crosses chronological, geographic, confessional, and genre divisions. The earliest was most likely written within a few years of Muḥammad's death, the latest toward the end of the Umayyad dynasty, in the mid-eighth century. Their authors lived in lands that constitute present-day Turkey, Lebanon, Jordan, Syria, Iraq, and Iran. They were written by Miaphysites, Maronites, and East Syrian Christians. They include apocalypses, caliph lists, conciliar decisions, chronicles, colophons, disaster lists, disputations, encyclical letters, epistles, flyleaf scribblings, hagiographies, inscriptions, legal opinions, and scriptural exegesis. What unites these diverse documents is how important they all are for ancient as well as modern images of Christian-Muslim interactions and of early Islam.

Because Syriac Christians were among the first to meet Muslims, their records of such encounters remain particularly important for the history of Christian-Muslim relations. This does not mean that Syriac texts objectively describe moments of first contact. But they have preserved some of the earliest impressions and portrayals of Muslims. They were at the forefront of Christian constructions of Islam.

These Syriac images of Islam are especially valuable because Syriac writings came from a much different perspective than Byzantine and Latin sources. Since within a few years after Muḥammad's death Syriac Christians were under Islamic control, unlike Byzantine and Latin authors, most Syriac Christians were not writing from the context of active military conflict.

Living in the Islamic Empire, they also had much greater contact with Muslims and a more direct knowledge of Islam. Syriac Christians ate with Muslims, married Muslims, bequeathed estates to Muslim heirs, taught Muslim children, and were soldiers in Muslim armies.

These direct interactions did not result in uniformly positive images of Islam. Syriac texts do not suggest that early Christian-Muslim relations were a paragon of harmony and coexistence. But the incredible diversity of Syriac depictions, ranging from overtly antagonistic to downright friendly, also belies a solely hostile reaction. These texts remind us that Christians' and Muslims' first interactions were not characterized by unmitigated conflict.

At the same time, Syriac texts remain an important, and often underused, resource for better understanding early Islam. There are few Islamic documents besides the Qur'an itself that scholars can securely date to within a century of Muḥammad's death. Thousands of pages of Islamic sources describing the time from Muḥammad up to the end of the Umayyad dynasty in 750 survive, but almost all of these were written under the subsequent dynasty of the Abbasids. Few doubt that these later works contain at least some accurate accounts. No one, however, has successfully separated authentic early traditions from later interpolations. If historians rely solely on Arabic texts, they remain almost entirely dependent on documents written centuries after the events that they depict.

Islam, however, is unusual among world religions in having its origins more thoroughly documented by outsiders than by insiders. Dozens of seventh- and early eighth-century Christian texts refer to Islam. Describing Islam from the outside, these works have their own agendas and biases. Nevertheless, they contain a treasure trove of data essential for better understanding the first Islamic century.

The value of this perspective can perhaps best be appreciated by analogy. Scholars of early Christianity face a somewhat similar dilemma to that of early Islam scholars. There is only a small corpus of surviving first- and early second-century Christian writings, primarily found in what later became the canonical New Testament. Most surviving early Christian texts were not written until the mid-second and early third centuries. Scholarship thus often turns to early non-Christian sources.

For example, there is hardly an undergraduate class offered on early Christianity whose syllabus does not include the two pages that the early second-century pagan author Pliny the Younger wrote about Christians. Virtually every New Testament textbook includes a discussion of the one paragraph referring to Jesus found in the late first-century *Antiquities of the Jews.* New Testament scholars continue to vigorously debate whether these few sentences were actually written by the Jewish historian Josephus or were a later Christian interpolation. So too the handful of sentences by the Roman historian Tacitus that speak of Christianity remains central to all scholarship on Roman persecution of Christians.

The sum total of these early, outsider references to Christians is less than five pages. In contrast, there are almost two hundred pages' worth of very early Syriac references to Islam. Historians and students of early Islam must use such passages with great care. Outsider literature is no less biased than insider literature. Syriac authors had their own agendas and vary substantially in their historical reliability. Nevertheless, one can only imagine the impact a similar quantity of material would have on the study of early Christianity.

If used critically, these early Syriac references to Islam may have a lot to tell us. They not only preserve an invaluable record of the earliest Christian images of Muslims. They are also highly significant for our own understanding and images of earliest Islam.

630s −750

When Christians First Met Muslims includes almost all known Syriac texts that most scholars think were composed before the Abbasid revolution in 750 and that explicitly refer to Muslims, Islam, the Islamic conquests, or the direct circumstances of Islamic rule, such as the poll tax. I have chosen to organize these texts in as close to chronological order as current scholarship allows. One could quite profitably group them by genre, by confessional affiliation, or by some other heuristic. Chronological order, however, has the advantage of highlighting the often strong correlation between the changing circumstances of Syriac Christians and their depictions of Islam.

No surviving Syriac sources written prior to the death of Muḥammad (ca. 632) speak of Islam. But just a few years after his death, during the period of his first four successors, known as the Rashidun, or "rightly guided," caliphs (632−61), several Syriac authors noted their experiences under Islam. It is extremely unusual to have ancient, outsider accounts written so close to the beginning of a new religious movement. Although such references are brief, they are particularly valuable.

The earliest surviving Syriac reference to Islam, the *Account ad 637*, was most likely written as the Islamic conquests were unfolding. The *Chronicle ad 640*, from only a few years later, also briefly speaks of the conquests. In addition to helping one better understand the military history of the time, both these sources are remarkable in referring to Muḥammad, and they indicate how quickly Syriac Christians were aware of his centrality to the emergence of Islam. Neither source, however, attributes any particular religious beliefs to the new conquerors. Both refer to them simply as *ṭayyāyē*, which was the most typical Syriac word for "Arabs" but, at the time, was not limited to followers of any given religion.

A decade later, the head of the East Syrian Church, Catholicos Isho'yahb III, referred to Muslims in a couple of his extant letters. His brief allusions to Muslims and Muslim rule are particularly good examples of political expediency. Isho'yahb generally seemed much more interested in keeping his bishops in line than in Islam. He referenced Christians converting to Islam as an example of why his least favorite bishop should be seen as particularly inept. In order to reprimand another set of bishops, he mentioned that Muslims honored and aided the church. When speaking about Muslim leaders, he reminded his audience of Jesus's command to render unto Caesar what is Caesar's. He also presented the first of many examples of Syriac clergy trying to use Muslim rule for the benefit of their own branch of Syriac Christianity and to the detriment of competing Syriac churches. Overall, Isho'yahb devoted only one or two dozen sentences to Islam. And even these references, valuable though they are, were always in the context of his much greater concern for internal church politics. The scant attention these early authors paid to the rise of Islam may surprise modern readers. Yet it was perfectly understandable given their historical context. For seventh-century Syriac Christians, the most involved geopolitical changes came not with the Islamic conquests of the 630s but with the Byzantine-Persian war from 602 to 628, which was much more destructive than the Islamic conquests. In a period of just over thirty years, many Syriac Christians experienced no fewer than four changes of governance: Byzantine to Persian to Byzantine to Arab. Initially there was little reason to suppose that Arab rule would last any longer than its immediate predecessors. At first, Arab forces settled mainly in newly founded garrison towns; Islam generally did not proselytize non-Arabs; conversion rates among non-Arabs remained low; local governing structures were left almost completely intact; and even the poll tax seems to have been more a gradual expansion of previous revenue structures than a radically new burden. As a result, Syriac Christians first described what we call the Islamic conquests as though there was nothing explicitly Islamic about them, and what we see today as one of the world's most important interreligious encounters barely received mention from its contemporaries.

In the mid-650s, however, there was a decisive change in the political history of the Islamic Empire. In 656 the assassination of the caliph 'Uthmān ignited a succession crisis between his successors 'Alī and Mu'āwiya, the governor of Syria. In 661 this first Arab civil war (*fitna*) ended soon after 'Alī's assassination by the Khārijites, a group that had split off from his own. After 'Alī's death, Mu'āwiya founded the first Islamic dynasty. His family, the Umayyads, retained control of most of the Islamic Empire until 750.

Syriac sources written around the beginning of the Umayyad dynasty were quite varied. As before, some, like the *Khuzistan Chronicle,* look back to the Islamic conquests and provide important data about the battles fought. Others were much more impressionistic. For example, the *Apocalypse of Pseudo-Ephrem* contains a hundred-line poetic description of the Islamic conquests depicting them in the most horrific of terms and seeing them as the harbinger of the end times. Some sources, like the *Maronite Chronicle,* document the Syriac churches' continuing to jockey for power as they tried to gain Muslim support for their particular branch of Christianity. Other writings, such as rulings from an East Syrian synod convened in 676, allude to some of the everyday issues that arose under Muslim rule: Christians turning to Muslim courts to gain more advantageous decisions than they thought they could in ecclesiastical courts, Christian tax collectors demanding the poll tax from their bishops, and intermarriage between Christians and Muslims.

Syriac Christians were now referring to Islam in an increasingly diverse set of genres—historical chronicles, ecclesiastic letters, apocalypses, and conciliar decisions. They also continued to make an occasional allusion to Muḥammad or to issues we attribute to Islam, such as the importance of the Ka'ba. But none yet depicted what we call Islam as anything close to an independent religious tradition.

This began to change in 683 with the second civil war and its aftermath. Following the death of Mu'āwiya's grandson Mu'āwiya II, the Umayyad caliphs Marwān (r. 684–685) and his son 'Abd al-Malik (d. 705) fought a nine-year war against a rival caliph, 'Abd Allah ibn al-Zubayr (d. 692). This second fitna resulted in substantial casualties and threatened to tear apart the Islamic Empire. One of the few contemporary witnesses to these events whose writings survive was the East Syrian monk John bar Penkāyē. At the request of his abbot, John wrote a world history that culminated in the second civil war. In light of what he and his monastery were experiencing, he believed humanity had lost its last chance for reform. According to John, God had realized that nothing would now motivate humans to repent, so he had removed his heavenly care from the world, ushering in the beginning of the end.

John turned out to be wrong. Just a few years after he finished his lengthy chronicle, Ibn al-Zubayr was defeated in Mecca. In 692 'Abd al-Malik became the sole caliph, and his descendants would control the caliphate until 750. The end of the second fitna was not, however, an unmitigated blessing for Syriac Christians. The political stability following the second Arab civil war, along with 'Abd al-Malik's substantial building program, the minting of his own coins, a census, and tax reform, suggested that the Arab state was not going away anytime soon.

As the head of this state, 'Abd al-Malik began to champion Islam. Toward the end of the second fitna, Muslim proclamations of faith and polemics against Christian theology began to appear on milestones, coins, and, most prominently, the newly constructed Dome of the Rock. Built on the Temple Mount in Jerusalem and inscribed with Qur'anic passages decrying Trinitarian theology, the Dome of the Rock clearly pronounced 'Abd al-Malik's intention of proclaiming Islam a successor religion to Christianity. While he was increasing Islam's public prominence, the caliph also began to regulate public displays of Christianity, especially depictions of the cross. At the same time, he changed the language of governance, replacing a variety of local languages—such as Coptic, Greek, Persian, and Syriac—with an Arabophone administration. This helped begin a centuries-long process that eventually reduced Syriac from a lingua franca to a primarily liturgical language.

For Syriac Christians, the immediate literary response to these changing circumstances was a spate of apocalypses. Works such as the *Edessene Apocalypse,* the *Apocalypse of John the Little,* and the immensely popular *Apocalypse of Pseudo-Methodius* all stubbornly proclaimed the invincibility of the Byzantine Empire and the Muslims' imminent demise—a stance that contemporary events made increasingly untenable. For these authors, the conquerors' role as a short-lived scourge of Christian sins completely overshadowed their beliefs and practices.

Writing at the same time as his more apocalyptically inclined brethren, Jacob, the Miaphysite bishop of Edessa, provided a much different perspective on life under 'Abd al-Malik. Of particular import are his letters, which often preserve a much more on-the-ground viewpoint of Christian-Muslim interactions than those found in most other sources. Jacob reported extensive contact and a great deal of religious overlap between Christians and Muslims. His writings also reflect a more detailed knowledge of his conquerors' beliefs and practices than earlier sources do. Of all seventh-century authors, Jacob came the closest to depicting Islam as an independent religious tradition, albeit one with extremely ill-defined borders. This shift was undoubtedly related to the consolidation of Islamic identity under Umayyad rule and the caliphate's increased emphasis on religious promotion.

As the Umayyad dynasty further solidified under 'Abd al-Malik's successors, Christian hopes for a quick end to Arab rule soon fizzled. When apocalyptic expectations were not met, eighth-century Syriac writers had to develop other interpretive frameworks to address life under Islam. Eighth-century Umayyad caliphs expanded 'Abd al-Malik's project of Islamization. Particularly significant was the reign of 'Abd al-Malik's nephew 'Umar II (r. 718–20). As caliph, he began to assess taxes not on the basis of lineage but on the basis of religion. Prior to this, the main way to be exempt from the poll tax was to be born an Arab. In most cases, even the process of becoming the client of an Arab sponsor and then joining the Muslim community did not result in a change of tax status. That is, the poll tax was tied primarily to natal, not religious, affiliation. Although his policy changes were not consistently implemented until well after his death, 'Umar II declared non-Arab converts exempt from the poll tax. From this point on, the caliphate presented a religion that, at least in theory, transcended ethnic difference. 'Umar II may also have begun a series of evolving regulations that tried to more clearly distinguish Muslims from non-Muslims. In later centuries, this increasingly discriminatory legislation was consolidated into the so-called Pact of Umar.

As their conquerors' religion was becoming both more assertive and—in terms of its self-presentation—less exclusively tied to ethnicity, Syriac Christians more frequently distinguished themselves from their conquerors through the categories of religion and religious difference. Particularly important was the emergence of disputation texts like the *Disputation of John and the Emir* and the *Disputation of Bēt Ḥalē*, which each describe an alleged debate between a Christian and a high-status Muslim interlocutor.

The very choice to write in this genre tells much about Syriac Christians' changing views of their conquerors. Such disputations, both in real life and in literature, almost always occurred between proponents of competing religious traditions. By discussing Muslim beliefs and practices in the framework of a disputation, the authors of *John and the Emir* and the *Disputation of Bēt Ḥalē* implicitly gave them the categorical status of a religion—more specifically, a religion that threatened Christian orthodoxy. Other Syriac sources from this time, such as fragments from the writings of Ḥnanishoʿ I and Mār Abbā II, provide further evidence of an increased awareness of Islamic beliefs and practices that differed from Christian ones.

Umayyad-era Syriac sources reflect radical changes in the ways Christians thought about, wrote about, and categorized their conquerors during the first century after the conquests. Developments in terminology, level of detail, narrative context, choice of genre, and even length of presentation suggest that later generations of Syriac Christians were increasingly inclined to construct their conquerors' beliefs and practices as constituting a categorical entity (what we call Islam). They became more familiar with their conquerors' doctrines and more specifically defended Christianity against its challenges. In the latter part of the Umayyad era, Syriac authors also began to designate their conquerors more explicitly as having a religion, albeit one whose boundaries with Christianity remained quite porous and hard to define.

By the mid-eighth century, authors of all genres of Syriac literature had developed areas of rough consensus for how to portray their conquerors' beliefs and practices. The terminology that Umayyad-era writers developed, their growing knowledge base regarding Muslims, their inclination to more directly address Muslim polemics, and their tendency to attribute religious characteristics to the conquerors served as the foundation for all later Syriac texts about Islam.

In 747 the Abbasid family led a revolt against Umayyad rule. Three years later they defeated the Umayyad caliph Marwān II, took control of most of the Islamic Empire, and established the Abbasid dynasty. A plethora of Islamic texts survive from early in this period. Syriac sources written in the Abbasid era remain essential for understanding how non-Muslims viewed Muslim rule and for the history of early Christian-Muslim relations. But with the rise of a robust Muslim historiographic tradition and with greater chronological distance from the events that they depicted, these later Syriac authors are often seen as less central than their predecessors for understanding earliest Islam.

NAVIGATING *WHEN CHRISTIANS FIRST MET MUSLIMS*

A quick perusal of more than a century of Syriac writings on Islam provides some historical context for these works, isolates a few major trends of their authors, and hints at several reasons why they are so important for our knowledge of late antiquity and the early Middle Ages. But such a cursory overview certainly does not do justice to the richness and complexity of these works, nor does it indicate all the ways they can add greater nuance to how we understand early Islam. For that, it is necessary to read the texts themselves.

When Christians First Met Muslims provides three resources to help one navigate this corpus. First are the brief introductions to each text. Because I have analyzed these documents' contents more extensively elsewhere, my introductions here aim to provide only the most basic source-critical information to help orient the modern reader. This includes a brief discussion of the text's import to the study of early Islam, the state of its preservation within extant manuscripts, and arguments concerning its provenance, with a particular focus on the likely composition date and the author's confessional affiliation.

Second, those who want to do more in-depth research of a given work will find at the end of *When Christians First Met Muslims* bibliographies corresponding to each text. These citations are heavily indebted to the bibliographic projects of my predecessors but also include more recent publications. For less studied texts, these bibliographies are meant to be fairly inclusive.

For the few Syriac works that have been more extensively researched, I limit the bibliographies to some of the most influential and some of the more recent studies.

Third, with the exceptions of the *Life of Theodutē* and the *Disputation of Bēt Halē*, which others soon will publish in translation, my own translation of the text follows each introduction. Here I am in great debt to those scholars who have painstakingly produced editions and prior translations of most of these works. Their labor has kept me from a myriad of errors. My decision to produce my own translations is not a critique of their work. It simply seems desirable to provide a fairly unified style of translation across documents.

My goal to have as large an audience as possible read and study these works has substantially affected how I translated them. As a translator I have presumed that historians engaged in the in-depth, specialized study of an individual document will always read that text in the original language. To help such specialists, I have included in the margins page numbers from the editions I have used, so that they can quickly coordinate my English translation with the Syriac text. The purpose of this volume, however, is to provide an entryway into early Syriac writings on Islam, often for those who do not read Syriac. For this purpose, I am much more invested in providing readable prose than in producing a mirror translation of the Syriac.

This results in certain trade-offs. Most important, I do not always translate a Syriac word into the same English word throughout the corpus. Even though there would be benefits to such consistency, most Syriac words have a range of semantic meanings, and at times context and idiom require different words in English. So too I occasionally use a given English word to render more than one Syriac term because there are places where Syriac vocabulary is simply more expansive than English.

Nevertheless, because of the book's focus I retain formal equivalence for one particular set of words. By the 750s there had not yet emerged a word corresponding to our term *Islam*. Instead, Syriac sources used a variety of terms to describe people whom we would call Muslims. None of these were identical to our word *Muslim,* and their connotations not only varied between texts but also developed over time. To help trace this evolution I translate each of these Syriac terms with only one English word and reserve that English word for the corresponding Syriac term. These one-for-one correspondences are "Arab" for *ṭayyāyā,* "Arabian" for *'arabāyā,* "Hagarene" for *mhaggrāyā* (and its alternate spellings), "Ishmaelite" for *'Ishma'elāyā,* "Saracene" for *sarqāyā,* "Son of Hagar" for *bar Hāgār,* and "Son of Ishmael" for *bar 'Ishma'el.* I have also rendered the Syriac term for a polytheist (*ḥanpā*) as "pagan," even though later texts derogatorily apply this term to Muslims.

To avoid good Syriac sounding like bad English, I have also employed the types of transformations that most translators of Syriac use. I have often dropped the nearly ubiquitous "and" (*wa*) from the start of many Syriac sentences. I have occasionally converted a dependent into an independent clause to avoid half-page-long sentences that work fine in Syriac but inevitably become awkward in English. I have sometimes made a passive sentence active to avoid stilted English. For Syriac idioms that have a clear English equivalent I have often used a similar English phrase, even if it is not identical word for word. I have also occasionally changed word order to clarify an antecedent. In general, however, I have kept such interventions more minimal than those found in most dynamic translations, and the English remains fairly close to the Syriac. Because Syriac normally does not include vowels for proper names, I have translated the most common (e.g., John) directly into English and for the names of Arabic rulers have used Arabic transliteration (e.g., Muḥammad). Less well-known names and places I have maintained in Syriac transliteration, adding vowels in those cases when the referent is obvious, preserving only the consonantal structure when it is not. I have also left untranslated the Syriac honorific Mār, as something like "my lord" or "sir" is simply too awkward in English.

The combination of basic introductions, detailed bibliographies, and accessible translations should help specialists and nonspecialists alike. As the largest and most diverse collection of early Christian writings about Islam, these texts certainly deserve a broad audience. Their perspective of seeing Islam from the outside provides invaluable information about the first Islamic century and the earliest interactions of the modern world's two largest faith communities.

Account ad 637

Most likely Miaphysite
Most likely ca. 637 C.E.

Probably the earliest, clearly the most dramatic, and arguably the most frustratingly incomplete of early Syriac references to the rise of Islam was likely written in 637. At that time, an anonymous author used a blank page in the front of his Bible to jot down a brief commemoration of the events he had just seen. Like most ancient books, at some point this one lost its cover, leaving the note unprotected. As a result, the opening page has been substantially damaged, and the ink is often unreadable. Nevertheless, this five-by-nine-inch piece of parchment with poorly preserved jottings constitutes the world's oldest surviving artifact to mention Muḥammad and likely refers to the most important battle of the Islamic conquests.

MANUSCRIPT AND EDITIONS

British Library Additional 14,461 contains a Syriac translation of the Gospels of Matthew and Mark. On paleographic grounds, William Wright dated the original manuscript to the sixth century. The Gospel of Matthew begins on the codex's second page and thus left the first page blank. On this flyleaf appears the brief *Account ad 637*. Because of its fragmentary state of preservation, several scholars have produced editions of the text, including Theodor Nöldeke in 1875 and Ernest Walter Brooks in 1904. In 1993, Andrew Palmer published a partially transliterated version based on notes made by Sebastian Brock.

AUTHORSHIP AND DATE OF COMPOSITION

British Library Additional 14,461 appears to be a Miaphysite Bible, and the scribblings on its flyleaf most likely came from a Miaphysite. The note refers to a battle that took place near the town of Gabitha in August of the year ——seven (the first two numbers are not fully preserved but most likely were nine and four). The year 947 in the Seleucid calendar that most Syriac Christians used corresponds to 636 C.E. Indeed, in August 636, just south of Gabitha, Arab troops decisively defeated Byzantine forces in an engagement more commonly known as the Battle of Yarmuk. The author claims to have been an eyewitness to some of the events he describes, and at one point he explicitly uses the first person to state that "we saw ...." By the seventh century, Syriac Christians already had a tradition of using the opening blank pages in a Bible for writing commemorative notices. The combination of biblical flyleaf and messy handwriting lends credence to the text's authorial claims. Because the last line of partially preserved text refers to the year following the battle near Gabitha, most modern scholars date the note's composition to circa 637.

.   .   .

Because of its extremely poor state of preservation, the *Account ad 637* remains quite fragmentary. Below are two translations of the same text. The first more stringently reflects the manuscript's current state. This translation includes only those words that remain clear in the manuscript or are very easily reconstructed.

> ... Muḥammad ... [p]riest, Mār Elijah ... and they came ... and ... and from ... strong ... month ... and the Romans ... And in January... of Emesa received assurances for their lives. Many villages were destroyed through the killing by ... Muḥammad and many people were killed. And captives ... from the Galilee to Bēt ... Those Arabs camped by ... we saw ... everywhe[re] ... and the ... that they ... and ... them. On the tw[enty-si]xth of May, ... went ... from Emesa. The Romans pursued them ... on the tenth ... the Romans fled from Damascus ... many, about ten thousand. The following [ye]ar, the Romans came. On the twentieth of August in the year n[ine hundred and forty-]seven [636 C.E.] there assembled in Gabitha ... the Romans and many people were ki[lled], from the R[omans] about fifty thousand ... In the year nine hundred and for[ty-] ...

This second translation of the same text attempts to fill in a few of the lacunae. It includes in braces those words that other scholars have conjectured as likely to have been in the document prior to its decay.

> ... Muḥammad ... priest, Mār Elijah ... and they came ... and ... and from ... strong ... month ... and the Romans {fled} ... And in

January {the people} of Emesa received assurances for their lives. Many villages were destroyed through the killing by {the Arabs of} Muḥammad and many people were killed. And captives {were taken} from the Galilee to Bet... Those Arabs camped by {Damascus}. We saw ... everywhere ... and the {olive oil} that they {had brought} and ... them. On the twenty-sixth of May, {the *sacellarius*} went ... from Emesa. The Romans pursued them ... On the tenth {of August} ... the Romans fled from Damascus ... many, about ten thousand. The following year, the Romans came. On the twentieth of August in the year nine hundred and forty-seven [636 C.E.] there assembled in Gabitha ... the Romans and many people were killed, from the Romans about fifty thousand ... In the year nine hundred and forty-{eight} ...

Chronicle ad 640

Miaphysite

ca. 640 C.E.

The *Chronicle ad 640* is a lengthy Miaphysite text that starts with the birth of Adam and continues to the opening years of the Islamic conquests. It does not present these events in anything close to chronological order, even though it often refers to specific years or indictions, fifteen-year periods that Byzantine chroniclers often used. Its rapid transitions between disparate lists of disasters, bishops, biblical characters, ecclesiastical councils, topography, and military campaigns have led some scholars to characterize its author as completely insane and others to hypothesize an ingenious method to his madness. Regardless of their view on how he organized the *Chronicle ad 640*, most scholars have been impressed with the author's knowledge of the early seventh century. For example, in regard to the Byzantine-Persian wars, Byzantine and Armenian sources corroborate the majority of the early seventh-century battles and dates that the *Chronicle ad 640* lists.

This makes it particularly unfortunate that the author devoted only a few sentences to the Arabs and their conquests. Nevertheless, because these lines come from a man whom most scholars believe was contemporary with the events he described, they remain especially valuable. Most see the *Chronicle*'s reference to a battle near Gaza as an allusion to the Battle of Dāthin, the earliest military clash between Arab and Byzantine forces. Several scholars also cite the *Chronicle ad 640* as the first non-Muslim reference to explicitly speak of Muḥammad by name (although, in truth, the *Chronicle ad 637* is arguably a better candidate). It is also notable what the chronicler omits. Despite a reference to military battles and civilian casualties, the author provides no explicitly religious explanation for these events. Unlike in later texts, here the conquests are neither a punishment for Christian sin nor a harbinger of the world's imminent end. So too the dearth of space the author dedicates to discussing the Arabs suggests that at least some of their contemporaries did not yet see the Islamic conquests as a world-changing event.

MANUSCRIPT AND EDITION

The *Chronicle ad 640* appears in a unique copy preserved in *British Library Additional* 14,643. The codex has lost ten of its first eleven folios but afterward remains complete. The extant text of the *Chronicle ad 640* takes up the first fifty-six of these sixty surviving folios. It is followed by a short caliph list now known as the *Chronicle ad 724*. The manuscript's last pages contain a brief colophon in the handwriting of the original scribe and some hymns added by a later hand. On paleographic grounds, William Wright estimated that this manuscript was written in the mid-eighth century. Ernest Walter Brooks published an edition of the text in 1904.

AUTHORSHIP AND DATE OF COMPOSITION

Several details enable a fairly secure dating of this *Chronicle*, especially its entries that speak of the Islamic conquests. Its last dated entry is from about 635/36. The only allusion to a time later than that is a brief reference to the emperor Heraclius's having reigned for thirty years. This would correspond to 640. The author also ends a list of Byzantine emperors with Heraclius but does not mention his death, which occurred in 641, nor the accession of any subsequent emperors. This all suggests that Heraclius was still alive when the *Chronicle* was written and points to a composition date around 640.

Most scholars believe that the scribe who produced *British Library Additional* 14,643 copied down an already completed chronicle and then simply added an eighth-century caliph list immediately afterward. According to this view, what is now called the *Chronicle ad 640* represents a fairly unified, almost completely preserved single-author work, all of which is securely dated to the mid-seventh century. Recently, however, James Howard-Johnston has argued for a more complicated transmission history. He suggests that, far from simply copying down an earlier work, the mid-eighth-century scribe of *BL Add.* 14,643 composed a new one (what we erroneously call the *Chronicle ad 640*) from five different sources, only one of which was written around 640. For this reason, Howard-Johnston refers to the work found in *BL Add.* 14,643 not as the *Chronicle ad 640* but rather as the *Chronicle ad 724*. If he is correct, this would have important implications for the overall structure and literary history of the

Chronicle. Fortunately, the text's brief references to the Islamic conquests occur in the section of the work that all modern scholars, including Howard-Johnston, date to circa 640.

As several parts of the *Chronicle* defend an explicitly Miaphysite Christology and view of history, the theological affiliation of its author is quite obvious. In the section translated below, the author makes a brief reference to the death of the doorkeeper Simon, the brother of Thomas the priest. Because Simon plays no other role in the narrative, many suggest that the *Chronicle*'s author is none other than this Thomas. As a result, the *Chronicle* is sometimes called the *Chronicle of Thomas the Presbyter.*

. . .

In the year 945 [634 c.e.], the seventh indiction, on Friday, February the fourth, at the ninth hour, there was a battle between the Romans and the Arabs of Muḥammad in Palestine, twelve miles east of Gaza. The Romans fled. They abandoned the patrician *Bryrdn,* and the Arabs killed him. About four thousand poor villagers from Palestine—Christians, Jews, and Samaritans—were killed, and the Arabs destroyed the whole region.

In the year 947 [635/36 c.e.], the ninth indiction, the Arabs invaded all Syria and went down to Persia and conquered it. They ascended the mountain of Mardin, and the Arabs killed many monks in Qedar and Bnātā. The blessed Simon, the doorkeeper of Qedar, the brother of Thomas the priest, died there.

Letters

ISHO'YAHB III

East Syrian

ca. 650 C.E.

Isho'yahb III (d. 659) had an impeccable ecclesiastical lineage. Born to a noble family in Abiabene, he became a monk under the first abbot of the famous East Syrian monastery of Bēt 'Abē, then progressed through the successively more prestigious offices of bishop, metropolitan, and catholicos, the head of the East Syrian church, which he became in the last decade of his life. During his ecclesiastical career, Isho'yahb wrote numerous epistles detailing the day-to-day operation of the Church of the East in the first decades of Islam. None of the 106 of his surviving letters focus solely on Islam. But three include passages that are particularly important for witnessing some of the earliest interactions between Christians and Muslims.

Letter 48B concentrates on intra-Christian rivalry between monks under Isho'yahb's jurisdiction and Miaphysites ("those who attributed suffering and death to God"). Here Isho'yahb chastises the East Syrian monks for showing insufficient zeal. He argues that the Hagarene Arabs did not innately favor Miaphysites and, in any cases when they did, with a little effort could be persuaded to support the East Syrian cause instead. This letter presents the earliest example of a larger trend among Syriac writings. When Syriac Christians spoke of dealings with their conquerors, the authors' main concern was rarely Christianity's encounter with another religion. Instead, the discussion often focused on how to get their conquerors to support one branch of Christianity over another. This letter is also important because of its terminology. It includes the earliest surviving employment of the word *Hagarenes* (*mhaggrāyē*), which eventually became one of the most common that Syriac authors used to speak of Muslims. In this case Isho'yahb uses the word to specify that he is speaking not of Arabs in general but rather of those Arabs who are also Hagarenes. Some scholars have suggested that the passage's progression of usages, from *Arab* to *Hagarene Arabs* to simply *Hagarenes,* reflects Isho'yahb's attempt to introduce his audience to a relatively new term.

In *Letter* 14C Isho'yahb does not use the term *Hagarene* but rather speaks of "Arabs to whom at this time God has given control over the world." The letter as a whole, however, does not focus on Muslims at all. Rather, Isho'yahb addressed his *Letter* 14C to Simeon, the metropolitan bishop of Rev Ardashir, who was attempting to secede from the catholicos's authority. In response, Isho'yahb sent a sharp reprimand, including a lengthy list of the alleged shortcomings of Christians under Simeon's jurisdiction. Of particular note are Isho'yahb's allegations that most of Simeon's congregations were apostatizing. Isho'yahb stresses that such apostasy is inexcusable. According to him, the Arabs were generally supportive of Christians and allowed them to keep their faith. Simeon's congregants were deserting Christianinty simply to avoid the Arabs' demand for half their possessions. Modern scholars have frequently cited this passage for diametrically opposed reasons. In general they emphasize either the beginning, to illustrate Muslim authorities' general benevolence toward Christianity, or the conclusion, to illustrate Muslim discrimination against Christians, in this case a 50 percent poll tax (otherwise unattested) on non-Muslims. The often unacknowledged difficulty of either interpretation is Isho'yahb's own agenda. The goal of his letter was not an accurate description of Christianity in the Persian Gulf (a topic about which he may have had at best indirect knowledge). Rather, he wanted to portray his subordinate bishop and personal nemesis in as negative a light as possible.

In *Letter* 15C Isho'yahb is again on the offensive, in this case writing against the bishops of Bēt Qaṭrayē, who were also questioning his authority. As one of his arguments for the necessity of centralized control, he presents himself as an important intercessor between Christians and their Arab rulers. In this context, he provides one of the earliest surviving references to Christians under Islam paying a poll tax.

Isho'yahb's discussions of Muslims are brief and, given their polemical context, difficult to assess. Nevertheless, written less than two decades after the Islamic conquests, his *Letters* remain essential witnesses for how the first generation of Christians under Islamic rule were experiencing and interpreting its early days.

MANUSCRIPTS AND EDITION

The oldest extant copy of Isho'yahb's *Letters* appears in *Vatican Syriac* 157, which has been dated to the tenth century on paleographic grounds. The letters are also found in a number of more modern manuscripts, including *Chaldean Patriarchate* 112 (1696), *Mardin* 78 (1868), *Leeds Syriac* 4.1 (1888), *Alqosh* 172 (1894), *Baghdad Chaldean Monastery Syriac* 515 (1894), *Baghdad Chaldean Monastery Syriac* 516 (1901), *Baghdad Chaldean Monastery Syriac* 517 (1902), *Paris Syriac* 336 (1896), and *Vatican Syriac* 493 (1909). In 1905 Rubens Duval published an edition of the *Letters* based on *Vatican Syriac* 157 and *Paris Syriac* 336.

AUTHORSHIP AND DATE OF COMPOSITION

No one has contested the attribution of these letters to Isho'yahb III. Traditionally they have been divided into those written when Isho'yahb was the bishop of Nineveh-Mosul (628–ca. 637), when he was the metropolitan of Erbil (ca. 637–649), and when he was catholicos (649–659). The heading of *Letter* 48B claims that he wrote this epistle while bishop of Nineveh (and hence in the mid-to-late 630s). Most recent scholars, however, suggest that a later scribe misordered several of the letters, including 48B, which they say belongs to the period when Isho'yahb was a metropolitan or catholicos. As both their headings and their contents indicate, Isho'yahb clearly wrote *Letters* 14C and 15C in the last decade of his life, while he was catholicos.

.   .   .

[Letter] Forty-Eight [B]

Isho'yahb, the stranger, who by God's grace serves the holy church in Nineveh, to the fainthearted sons of the real believers and true Christians: Qāmisho', Sania, Babusa, Hnanisho', Isaac, Barsahde, and Dadiazd. By God, the omnipotent, may peace multiply among you.

93

Poor men, the evil of faithlessness that you alone happen to now suffer before the rest of the lost [will] threatens the world's fall and the destruction of men's lives. By this, that which had been said by our Lord concerning the present times has already been fulfilled in you: "When the Son of Man comes, will he find faith on the earth?" [Lk 18:8] ...

.... I also think that at this time your action is in greater need 96 of prayer than of a letter. Before God will visit you with the mercy of his grace, I, a sinner and a wretch, will also see you. I will make known how you are, how the good hope of your fathers' faith has been kept by you (if it has been kept), and whether you have fully repented for what happened—in short, whether you have completely lost Christian goodness. Even if it seems differently to others, I want to test you in this. For, by our Lord's word, you are not anywhere allowed to enter one of the churches and to partake in the divine mysteries until you bear the zeal of the faith of our Lord in your hearts, your tongues, and your hands, [until] you destroy those impure seals that, through a servant of his will, Satan placed upon the door of your church, and [until] you demonstrate righteous diligence for [the church]—to build it up, to increase it, to enrich it, to sanctify it—as is appropriate for the church of God.

And if it should happen that, making false excuses, you 97 should say (or that heretics should deceive you [into saying]) that what happened happened through the Arabs' command, [know that this] is completely untrue. For the Arab Hagarenes do not help those who attribute suffering and death to God, the Lord of all. If it should happen and for whatever reason they have helped them, if you properly attend to this, you can inform the Hagarenes and persuade them concerning this matter. Thus, my brothers, do everything wisely. Give what is Casesar's to

Caesar and what is God's to God. God most high, who is able to increase every benefit for those fearing him—he will perfect you with every good deed to always do his will all the days of your lives. Amen. [The letter] is finished.

[Letter] Fourteen [C]
To Simeon, the bishop of Rev Ardashir.

From Isho'yahb to our honored brother Mār Simeon, the metropolitan bishop of Rev Ardashir. Greetings in our Lord.

Our God-loving brother, at this time Your Holiness has bestowed upon us the meeting that appears in the spiritual law—even if, lover of good, in accord with your will's desire, [it was bestowed] not by [you] coming in person, as the spiritual law demands, but by sending a fellow minister [as] a representative and by [sending] a letter of greeting. When I read what you had written and also heard what you had sent, I rejoiced and thanked our Lord. But I not only rejoiced in what you wrote and sent, but also needed to feel sorrow at the evil reports that a little while earlier had come to me from the edges of your diocese. Through the necessity of reconciling [your letter] with the report [of others], I simultaneously [experienced] a surging of joy along with sorrow, and laughter along with weeping. For a long time I had waited to be informed by you concerning the terrible things that have taken place in this region over which you were set as the guard of spiritual Israel. And behold, not until now (and [truly], not even now) has Your Holiness written me concerning the sort of things that have wickedly occurred in your region....

.... I will not respond to Your Holiness in kind, [with] learned speech and falsely called elegy. Rather, in common mourning, in strong lamentation, I will ask Your Holiness: Where are your children, barren father? Where are your sanctuaries, weak priest? Where are the great people of *Mrwny'*, who, seeing neither sword nor fire nor torture, like mad men became captivated by the love of half of their property? The Sheol of apostasy has suddenly swallowed them, and they have been destroyed forever....

... But unlike those who have hope in God's church and the prayer of the holy ones, you have not even turned to God's church to make known your ruin and to ask for the help of the prayer of our Lord's holy ones. Rather, until now, without sense or feeling, you have awaited the ruin that has befallen you. Not even now, when you wrote me what you wrote, did you make known to me [even] one of these things.... 249

... By the hands [of the holy ones], our Lord also performed various miracles as a demonstration of the greatness of their faith in him. And also among [the holy ones] are those who by God's grace attain ecclesiastical ministry—I mean the bishopric, the metropolitanate, and the catholicate, as well as the other [ecclesiastical] authorities under them. Because of things like these, through God's grace Christianity's glory multiplies further day by day, the faith grows, the episcopate abounds, and God's glory is increased. 250

You alone of all the people of the earth have rejected all these things. Because of [your] estrangement from all of this, deceptive influence easily first took control of you, as [it also does] now. For this one, your seducer and the overthrower of your churches, had previously appeared to us in the land of Radan, a land with much more paganism than Christianity. But because of the glorious conduct of the Christians, not even those pagans were deceived by him. Rather, he was expelled from here as one despised. Not only did he fail to overthrow the 251 churches, but he [himself] was overthrown. But in your Persia, pagans and Christians accepted him. Through the consent and obedience of pagans and the stupor and silence of Christians, he did with them as he wished.

For also these Arabs to whom at this time God has given control over the world, as you know, they are [also here] with us. Not only are they no enemy to Christianity, but they are even praisers of our faith, honorers of our Lord's priests and holy ones, and supporters of churches and monasteries. Indeed, how did your people of *Mrwny'* abandon their faith on pretext of [the Arabs']? And this when, as even the people of *Mrwny'* say, the Arabs did not force them to abandon their faith but only told them to abandon half of their possessions and to hold on to their faith. But they abandoned their faith, which is eternal, and held on to half of their possessions, which are ephemeral. The faith that all peoples have always bought with the peril of their lives and through which they inherit eternal life, your people of *Mrwny'* did not even buy with half of their possessions....

Letter 15 [C]

.... The insane neither know nor understand that they also are subject to this worldly authority that now rules everywhere ....
For the fools do not even discern that we are commanded to give every authority whatever we owe him: that is, to whomever [is owed] the poll tax, the poll tax; to whomever [is owed] tribute, tribute; to whomever [is owed] reverence, reverence; and to whomever [is owed] honor, honor.

Apocalypse of Pseudo-Ephrem

Likely Miaphysite

Second half of the seventh century C.E.

Because the manuscript title "A memrā by the Syrian teacher, the holy Mār Ephrem, concerning the end, the consummation, the judgment, the punishment, Gog, Magog, and the Antichrist" is a bit unwieldy, modern scholars most often refer to this text by the shorter name *Apocalypse of Pseudo-Ephrem*. As this nomenclature suggests, its attribution to the most famous of Syriac writers, Ephrem the Syrian (d. 363), is clearly false. The *Apocalypse* is structured as a *memrā*, or verse homily, that follows the form traditionally attributed to Ephrem: paired couplets of seven-syllable lines. This 560-line poem begins with the war between Rome (that is, the Byzantine Empire) and Assyria (that is, the Persian Empire). Then it predicts that, due to Christians' iniquity, God will punish the Romans by raising up Hagar's descendants, whose pillage, destruction, and demands for tribute will devastate the land. Soon afterward, in response to the Sons of Hagar's wickedness, God will release the armies of Gog, Magog, and the other nations of the North (an allusion to Ezekiel 38–39) that Alexander the Great previously imprisoned. These eschatological nations will destroy the Sons of Hagar and, in turn, will be defeated by an angelic host, who will also reinstate the Romans. This second cycle of Roman rule will conclude with the coming of the Antichrist, the Eschaton, and the Last Judgment.

Although only a fifth of this poem discusses Muslims, it remains one of the most important sources for early Syriac Christian reactions to the Islamic conquests. It may also be the earliest extant Syriac apocalypse that mentions Islam. Of particular interest is the author's consistently negative depiction of the Sons of Hagar, whose eschatological role nevertheless remains underdeveloped here in comparison with other (and most likely slightly later) Syriac apocalypses.

MANUSCRIPTS AND EDITIONS

The *Apocalypse of Pseudo-Ephrem* is preserved in two manuscripts, *Vatican Syriac 566*, which is dated to 1472, and *Dublin Trinity College* B 5.19, which was composed circa 1625. In 1972 Edmund Beck published a critical edition based on these two manuscripts.

AUTHORSHIP AND DATE OF COMPOSITION

The *Apocalypse of Pseudo-Ephrem* provides few clues about its author's Christological affiliation. Because of the text's discussion of Byzantine wickedness, along with its brief reference to the cry of those persecuted, most scholars suggest a Miaphysite author. Others, however, maintain a Chalcedonian authorship. Assessing a likely date of composition is even more challenging and mostly relies on arguments from silence. Although the text was clearly written after the Islamic conquests, the question remains how long after them. The lack of details regarding Islam, the depiction of Hagar's descendants primarily as plunderers, and the silence concerning late seventh-century political developments, such as the second Arab civil war, all suggest a composition date before the mid-680s. Moreover, unlike later Syriac apocalypses, this one shows no awareness of the immensely popular *Apocalypse of Pseudo-Methodius,* which was likely written around 692 and whose apocalyptic schema dominates all other Syriac apocalypses. As a result, most scholars see the *Apocalypse of Pseudo-Ephrem* as the first extant Syriac apocalypse to deal with Islam. Others, though, have contended that its mention of the extraction of tribute constitutes an oblique reference to 'Abd al-Malik's tax reforms in the early 690s and argue for a late seventh-century date of composition, which would make *Pseudo-Ephrem* contemporary with most other early Syriac apocalypses that mention Islam.

· · ·

Next, a memrā by the Syrian teacher, the holy Mār Ephrem, concerning the end, the consummation, the judgment, the punishment, Gog, Magog, and the Antichrist.

Son who by his grace descended
    and became incarnate, for it pleased him
[who] willingly tasted death
    atop a piece of wood on Golgotha
My Lord, help me speak about
    the quakes that will be upon the earth
Men will fall upon one another

and nations destroy one another
Wickedness will grow strong in the world
    and iniquity multiply upon the earth
Righteous kings will die
    and iniquitous ones rise up in the land
Then justice will rise up
    and cry out to men
The side of the iniquitous will weigh down [the scale]
    and that of the chosen lighten
Then the spiritual ones will go forth
    and destroy the ends of the earth
My brothers, it will be as it is written:
    disaster everywhere
There will be famine on the earth
    and harsh quakes and strife
The dust will become drunk with blood
    and the earth defiled with iniquity
Countries will be devastated
    and walled cities swallowed by Sheol
Nation will rise against nation
    and kingdom against kingdom
Iniquity will reign over the land
61   and the abominable will persecute the holy
Men will publically apostatize
    and the left side profit
The sons of righteousness will be oppressed
    by the sons of the side of sin
Thus, my beloved,
    the last age will arrive
Behold, we will see signs
    as Christ declared to us

Kings will rise up against one another
  and afflictions be upon the land
Nations will attack nations
  and armies fall upon one another
Like the river Nile of Egypt
  that floods and overflows upon the land
Countries will prepare for war
  against the Roman Empire
Nations will attack nations
  and kingdom [be] against kingdom
The Romans will go from place to place
  in flight
The Assyrians will rule
  the Roman Empire
The fruits of their loins will be enslaved
  and [the Assyrians] abuse even their women
[The Assyrians] will sow as well as reap
  and plant fruit in the earth
They will acquire great wealth
  and bury treasure in the earth
Like the river Nile of Egypt
  that after having ascended again descends
The Assyrians will again descend from the land
  to their [own] country
The Romans too will hasten
  to their fathers' country
When wickedness has increased in the world
  and [the wicked] have defiled the land with fornication
A cry of the poor and persecuted
  will ascend to heaven
Then justice will rise up

to cast [the wicked] from the land
The voice of the holy ones will wail
and a cry ascend to heaven
A people there will go forth from the desert
the son[s] of Hagar, Sarah's maidservant
[A people] who uphold the covenant of Abraham,
the husband of Sarah and Hagar
They will be compelled to enter [the land] in the name of
the ram,
the emissary of the Son of Destruction
There will be a sign in heaven
as our Lord said in his gospel
A brilliance will be among the shining stars
the fire of its countenance aflame
Kings will quake and tremble
the battle lines of armies will fall
The people of the earth will become frightened
for they will see a sign in heaven
They will prepare for battle
and every people and every tongue will come together
There they will fight
and soak the earth with blood
There nations will be defeated
and a plundering people prevail
The plunderers will spread across the land
in valleys and on mountaintops
They will take women and children captive
as well as men, both elderly and youths
Men's beauty will be devastated
and women's adornment removed

With spears and strong lances
>they will pierce old men
They will separate a son from his father
>and a daughter from her mother's side
They will separate a brother from his brother
>and a sister from her sister's side
They will kill the bridegroom in his bedroom
>and expel the bride from her bridal chamber
They will take a wife from her husband
>and slaughter her like a lamb
They will cast an infant from his mother
>and drive the mother into captivity
The child will cry out from the earth
>his mother will hear, but what can she do?
For he will be trampled by the feet
>of horses, camels, and infantry
They will not allow her to turn toward him
>and the child will remain in the desert
They will separate children from [their] mother
>like a soul from the body
She will look at them while
>her beloved are torn from her lap
Two of her children to two masters
>she herself to another
Like her, her children will be divided
>to become slaves to captivity
Her offspring will cry out in anguish
>and their eyes gush tears
She will turn to her beloved
>milk overflowing from her breast

"Farewell, my beloved
    may God accompany you
He who accompanied Joseph
    into servitude among foreigners
will accompany you, my offspring
    into the captivity into which you go"
"Farewell, our mother
    and may God accompany you
He who accompanied Sarah
    [into] the household of Abimelech the Gerarite
will accompany you
    until the day of resurrection"
A son will stand and look at his father
    as he is sold into servitude
Their tears will gush
    in anguish, one before the other
63   A brother will see his brother
    killed and cast upon the earth
He too they will lead into captivity
    to become a slave in a foreign land
Mothers also will be killed
    their offspring clinging to their breasts
The voice of babes will mix
    with an anguish-filled groan
They will prepare roads in the mountains
    and paths in the valleys
They will plunder the ends of the earth
    and seize control of the cities
Countries will be devastated
    and the slain multiply upon the earth

All peoples will be humbled
    before a plundering people
When they have remained in the land a long while and
    people think
    "Behold, peace is coming"
They will exact tribute
    and everyone will fear them
Iniquity will multiply upon the land
    and obscure even the clouds
Wickedness will grow thick upon the land
    go up, and ascend to heaven
Then the Lord, on account of his anger
    at wickedness having multiplied upon the land
Will stir up the kings and the powerful armies
    whom he sends when he seeks to obliterate the earth
Men against men
    to destroy one another
Then justice will summon
    the kings and the powerful armies
Who are within those gates
    that Alexander had made
Behind the gates
    many kings and nations will rise up
They will look to heaven
    and call upon God's name
The Lord will send the sign
    of his glory from heaven
A divine voice will cry out
    to those within these gates
Immediately [the gates] will be overthrown and fall

at his divine command
Many armies will go forth
innumerable like the stars
64 As many as the sands of the sea
more than the stars of heaven ...

Khuzistan Chronicle

East Syrian

ca. 660 C.E.

One of the most valuable East Syrian chronicles is both anonymous and incompletely preserved. Because of its focus on the
region of Khuzistan, most scholars call this mid-seventh-
century work the *Khuzistan Chronicle*. It focuses on ecclesiastical
history from circa 590 to the mid-seventh century and twice
discusses Islam: once in the main section and a second time in a
section that most scholars suggest was written by a slightly more
recent author and then appended to the main work. These pages
contain some of the most extensive East Syrian descriptions of
the Islamic conquests and are especially important for those
trying to reconstruct seventh-century military history. They
also include references to Muḥammad, relations between Christian and Ishmaelite authorities, the Ka'ba, and Medina, as well
as the claim that God gave the Sons of Ishmael victory over the
Byzantines and the Persians.

MANUSCRIPTS AND EDITION

Four manuscripts preserve the *Khuzistan Chronicle: Baghdad, Chaldean Monastery 509, Vatican Borg. Syriac 82, Mingana Syriac 47,* and *Mingana Syriac 586.* The Baghdad manuscript is dated on paleographic grounds to the thirteenth or fourteenth century, the Vatican manuscript is from the nineteenth century, and the two Mingana manuscripts were copied in the early twentieth century. In 1903 Ignatius Guidi published an edition based on *Vatican Borg. Syriac 82,* which appears to be a modern copy from the medieval Baghdad manuscript.

AUTHORSHIP AND DATE OF COMPOSITION

The last fifth of the *Khuzistan Chronicle* witnesses an abrupt change in style and emphasis. These pages consist of more disparate sections without a clear narrative arc and focus more on secular events and issues of geography than do the earlier parts of the *Chronicle.* This narrative shift has led most scholars to suggest that these final pages form an appendix added to the original *Chronicle.* As a result, most modern scholars assign two composition dates to the surviving document. The main chronicle discusses the Islamic conquests for only a paragraph. What most scholars consider the appendix contains a much more extensive discussion of these conquests, as well as a brief discussion of the Ka'ba and of Medina.

The *Chronicle*'s main section relates events from the 590s to the 650s. Although it is anonymous, some modern scholars have suggested that Elias, the East Syrian metropolitan of Merv, could have been the author of at least this part of the work. Because it makes no allusion to any events after the 650s, whether they accept Elias as the author or not, most modern scholars suggest a composition date in the 650s or soon afterward. The last section, however, may allude to Elias's death (659). It also contains a statement that the Arabs have not yet conquered Constantinople. Some scholars have suggested that this constitutes an allusion to the siege of Constantinople in the late 670s, while others see it as a reference to the Arabs' first attack on Constantinople, in the 650s. As a result, those scholars who suggest that the last pages came from a different author than the writer of the rest of the chronicle date the composition of the "appendix" to several years after the main work, with estimates ranging from the 660s to the 680s. The entire document's focus on the Church of the East clearly witnesses East Syrian authorship.

. . .

In the city of Istakhr, they made Yazdgard from the royal lineage the king. With [Yazdgard] the kingdom of the Persians [would] end. He set out and came to Maḥuzē and appointed a general named Rustam. Then God brought against them the Sons of Ishmael, [who were as numerous] as sand upon the seashore. Their leader was Muḥammad. Neither walls nor gates nor armor nor shield withstood them. They took control of the entire Persian Empire. Yazdgard sent countless troops against them, and the Arabs destroyed all of them and also killed Rustam. Yazdgard confined himself within the walls of Maḥuzē, eventually escaped by flight, and went to the lands of the Huzāyē and the Marunayē. There his life ended. The Arabs took control of Maḥuzē and the entire region. They also went to the Roman Empire. They plundered and destroyed all the lands of Syria. And Heraclius, the king of the Romans, sent troops against them. The Arabs killed more than one hundred thousand of them. When the catholicos Isho'yahb saw that Maḥuzē had been destroyed by the Arabs, that they had carried off its gates to 'Aqulā, and that those remaining there were wasting away through hunger, he went to Bēt Garmai and dwelled in the village of Karkā.

Cyriacus of Nisibis died. Because of the Nisibites' hatred of him, they denounced his students before the city's emir. He summoned [them] and imprisoned them.

... Isho'yahb had led the patriarchate for eighteen years. His body was placed in the martyrium of the church of Karkā in Bēt Garmai. And Mār'ameh was appointed patriarch in the church. He was from the region of Arzun, from the town of Zuzimar. He had been appointed the metropolitan of Bēt Lapāṭ, and [earlier]

32 he had worn the monastic habit at the monastery of Mār Abraham of Izla. He had been greatly praised for his monasticism and as the metropolitan. Once he had been appointed the light of the Catholicate, he was honored by all the leaders of the Ishmaelites ...

35 ... And, at the aforementioned time when the Arabs had conquered all the lands of the Persians and the Romans, they also invaded Bēt Ḥuzāyē. They conquered all the fortified cities: that is Bēt Lapāṭ, Karkā d-Ledān, and the fortress of Shushan. But there remained Shush and Shushtrā, which were substantially fortified. However, from among all the Persians, none remained to resist the Arabs except for King Yazdgard and one of his generals, a Mede named Hormizdān, who had assembled troops and held Shush and Shushtrā.

36 The area of Shushtrā is very large and further fortified by strong rivers and canals that surround it on all sides, like moats. One of [the rivers] is called Ardashiragān, after the name of Ardashir, who had dug it. There is another that crosses it called

Shamirām, after the name of the queen. Another [is called] Dārāyagān, after the name Darius. The greatest of all of them is a strong torrent that descends from the northern mountains.

Then there went up against Hormizdān the Mede a general of the Arabs named Abū Mūsā, who, as a settlement for the Arabs, had built Baṣrā where the Tigris flows into the great sea. And [Baṣrā] is situated between cultivated land and desert, just as Saʿd bar Waqqās had built another settlement for the Arabs, the city ʿAqulā. [This city] was named Kūfā, after the name of the bend [*kpiputā*] in the Euphrates.

When Abū Mūsā went up against Hormizdān, Hormizdān devised ways to prevent [the Arabs] from [engaging in] battle with him until he had assembled an army. He informed Abū Mūsā that should he restrain himself from taking captives and [using] the sword, [Hormizdān] would send him however much tribute they imposed. So it remained for two years. But then Hormizdān's confidence in the walls broke the truce between them. [Hormizdān] killed those people conveying messages between them (including George, the bishop of Ulay), imprisoned Abraham, the metropolitan of Furāt, and sent many troops against the Arabs. The Arabs destroyed all of them and assailed and besieged Shush. In a few days they had conquered it and killed all the nobles there. They seized the house in it called the House of Mār Daniel. They took the treasure that, in accord with the commandments of kings, had been kept there from the days of Darius and Cyrus. They broke open and took the silver coffin in which was laid an embalmed body that many said was Daniel's, and others King Darius's.

They also besieged Shushtrā and for two years tried to seize it. Then, from among the foreigners, a Qaṭari man there befriended a man whose house was on the wall. The two of them conspired,

37

went out to the Arabs, and said to them, "If you give us a third of its plunder we will let you into the city." They made an agreement between themselves, dug holes under the walls from the inside, and let in the Arabs. [The Arabs] conquered Shushtrā, and there they poured out blood like water. They killed the city's interpreter and the bishop of Hormizd-Ardashir along with the rest of the students, priests, and deacons, whose blood they poured out [in] the sanctuary. But they seized Hormizdān alive.

Afterward, a man among the Arabs whose name was Kāled went west and seized cities and countries as far as 'Arab. Heraclius, the king of the Romans, heard [of this] and sent against them many armies, whose leader's name was *Sqylrā*. The Arabs defeated them, destroyed more than one hundred thousand of the Romans, and killed their leader. They also killed Isho'dād, the bishop of Ḥirtā, who was there with 'Abdmasiḥ while he served as an emissary between the Arabs and the Romans. The Arabs took control of all the lands of Syria and Palestine. They also wanted to enter Egypt but [initially] were unable to because the border was guarded by the patriarch of Alexander with a large and strong army. He had also blocked the land's entrances and exits and had built walls everywhere upon the Nile's shore. Due to [the walls'] height, the Arabs could enter [only] with difficulty. They seized the land of Egypt, Thebaid, and Africa.

38   Sorrow for the Romans' defeat overcame King Heraclius. He went up to his capital, grew sick, and died. He had reigned with his son for twenty-eight years.

The victory of the Sons of Ishmael who overcame and subjugated these two kingdoms was from God. Indeed, the victory is his. But God has not yet handed Constantinople over to them.

And concerning the Dome of Abraham, we could not find out what it is except for this. Because the blessed Abraham had became rich in property and also wanted to be far from the Canaanites' envy, he chose to dwell in the vast and distant parts of the desert. As a tent dweller, he built that place for God's worship and the offering of sacrifices. Because the place's memory had also been preserved by the clan's descendants, it took its current name from what it had been. It is not new for the Arabs to worship there. Rather, from their beginning, from long ago, [they have worshiped there,] paying honor to the forefather of their people.

And Haṣur, which scripture designates "the capital," is also the Arab's. [Theirs also are:] Medina, which is named after the name of Midian, Abraham's fourth son from Keturah (it is also called Yathrib); Dumat Gandal and the land of the Hagarites, which are rich in water, date palms, and fortified buildings; the land of Haṭṭā, which is situated near the sea in the vicinity of the islands of Qaṭar, similarly rich and filled with various plants; the land of Mazun, which, similar to [Haṭṭā], is also situated by the sea and [whose] area contains more than one hundred parasangs; the land of Yamāmā, which is in the middle of the desert; the land of Ṭup and the city of Ḥirtā, where King Murdar 39 resided, who was called the Warrior and was the Ishmaelites' sixth king.

The few notices from church history are finished.

Maronite Chronicle

Maronite

Possibly mid- to late seventh century C.E.

The title of this universal chronicle no longer survives. Due to the theological affiliation of its anonymous author, modern scholars most often refer to it as the *Maronite Chronicle*. Because only fragments remain, basic questions such as the work's composition date remain unresolved. Nevertheless, the *Chronicle*'s discussion of Islam, especially of Mu'āwiya's caliphate, is particularly valuable. In addition to providing data on mid-seventh-century military and political history, the *Maronite Chronicle* includes three particularly interesting episodes of interreligious encounter.

The first relates a debate between Miaphysites and Maronites that allegedly took place in front of the Umayyad caliph Mu'āwiya. According to the *Maronite Chronicle*, Mu'āwiya judged in favor of the Maronites and fined the Miaphysites. The Miaphysite patriarch, however, soon turned this to his advantage by continuing to pay Mu'āwiya to protect the Miaphysites from the Maronites. The next episode discusses Mu'āwiya's visit to Jerusalem, where he prayed at Golgotha, Gethsemane, and Mary's tomb. The text then refers to Mu'āwiya's issuing of gold and silver coins that broke from the widely used Byzantine coin type, no longer including the traditional depiction of the cross.

Although none of these anecdotes is innately implausible, scholars continue to debate their historical accuracy. Independent of their veracity, stories of a caliph who adjudicated intra-Christian debates and prayed at Christian holy sites but refused to mint coins with a cross remind one that the characters found in early Syriac sources often defy attempts to pigeonhole them into easily defined, mutually exclusive religious categories.

MANUSCRIPT AND EDITION

The *Maronite Chronicle* survives in a single, fragmentary manuscript. A flyleaf now housed in St. Petersburg contains the *Chronicle*'s beginning. The remaining leaves come from later folios in the *Chronicle* and are now found in the British Library, where they have been rebound as part of *British Library Additional* 12,216. On paleographic grounds, William Wright dated the manuscript to the eighth or ninth century. The extant sections begin in the time of Alexander the Great and continue until the mid-660s, although the discussion of the period between 361 and 658 no longer survives. With the exception of a missing leaf, *BL Add.* 12,216 does, however, preserve a continuous narrative from 658 until 665/66, when the manuscript breaks off prior to the *Chronicle*'s conclusion. In 1904 Ernest Walter Brooks published an edition of the surviving text.

AUTHORSHIP AND DATE OF COMPOSITION

The author's allegiance to the Maronites is made quite clear in the *Chronicle*. In its depiction of an intra-Christian debate before Caliph Mu'āwiya, the *Chronicle* champions "those of the faith of Mār Maron" and vilifies the Miaphysites. This has led some scholars to suggest that the author was the famed mid-eighth-century Maronite chronicler Theophilus of Edessa. More recent research on Theophilus has discredited this hypothesis, especially as there is no overlap between passages found in the *Maronite Chronicle* and the extensive fragments of Theophilus's *Chronicle* that later authors quote. As a result, the clear majority of scholars now consider the *Maronite Chronicle*'s author unknown.

Because the British Library manuscript breaks off in 665/66, there is no indication of how much further the *Chronicle* originally extended. Nevertheless, some scholars have forwarded several arguments suggesting a composition date not long after the 660s, including the facts that the *Chronicle* betrays no familiarity with the division between the Maronites and the Byzantine church, which took place in the early 680s, or their intensifying conflicts in the early eighth century; and that the proper correlation of specific dates and days of the week in the *Chronicle*'s last pages suggest that it was written by a near contemporary of the events it describes. Others have noted that the *Chronicle*'s dating of Christ's birth to the year 309 in the Seleucid calendar might betray a knowledge of Jacob of Edessa's *Chronicle*, which was not finished until the 690s. So too numismatists debate whether the *Chronicle*'s reference to Mu'āwiya's changing of Islamic coinage is plausible. Alternatively, it may be an anachronism based on the author's knowledge of 'Abd al-Malik's famous coin reform in the 690s. As a result, it remains uncertain whether the *Maronite Chronicle* was written in the mid-seventh century or simply comes from a somewhat later author well informed about the 660s.

.   .   .

... and Muʿāwiya, his nephew Ḥudaifa. Muʿāwiya issued a command concerning him and he was killed. Then ʿAlī also threatened to rise up against Muʿāwiya again. They struck him while he was praying at Ḥira and killed him. Muʿāwiya went down to 70 Ḥira, the entire Arab army there gave him allegiance, and he went back to Damascus.

In the year 970 [659 C.E.], the seventeenth year of Constans, at the second hour on a Friday in the month of June, there was a devastating earthquake in the land of Palestine, in which many places collapsed.

In the same month, the Jacobite bishops Theodore and Sabuk came to Damascus, and before Muʿāwiya they debated the faith with those of Mār Maron [i.e., the Maronites]. When the Jacobites were defeated, Muʿāwiya commanded them to give up twenty thousand denarii and be silent. And it became customary for the Jacobite bishops to give Muʿāwiya that [much] gold annually lest [his] protection of them slacken and they be punished by the [Maronite] clergy. He who was called patriarch by the Jacobites annually established what share of that gold the inhabitants of all the monasteries and convents would pay. Likewise, he established [the share] for the [other] followers of his faith. And he made Muʿāwiya heir [to his estate] so that out of fear of [Muʿāwiya] all the Jacobites would submit to him. On the ninth of the month during which the disputation with the Jacobites took place, at the eighth hour on a Sunday, [there was] an earthquake.

In the same year, the emperor Constans issued a command and his brother Theodosius was killed—wrongly, for he was innocent, as many say. Many were distressed by his murder. It is said that the citizens [of Constantinople] made public denunciations against the emperor and called him a second Cain, a committer of fratricide. Greatly angered, [Constans] left his son Constantine on the throne, took his queen and all the Romans' war-waging troops, and departed to the north against foreign peoples.

71

In the year 971 [660/61 c.e.], the eighteenth of Constans, many Arabs assembled in Jerusalem and made Muʿāwiya king. He ascended and sat at Golgotha. He prayed there, went to Gethsemane, descended to the tomb of the blessed Mary, and prayed there. In those days, while the Arabs were assembling there with Muʿāwiya, there was a tremor and a devastating earthquake. Most of Jericho collapsed, as did all of its churches. Mār John's house by the Jordon, where our savior was baptized, was uprooted from its foundations. So too the monastery of Abba Euthymius, along with the dwellings of many monks and solitaries, as well as many [other] places, collapsed during [the earthquake].

In the same year, in the month of July, the emirs and many [other] Arabs assembled and gave allegiance to Muʿāwiya. A command went out that he should be proclaimed king in all the villages and cities under his control and that they should make invocations and acclamations to him. He struck both gold and silver [coinage], but it was not accepted because it did not have a cross on it. Muʿāwiya also did not wear a crown like other kings in the world. He established his throne in Damascus but did not want to go to Muḥammad's throne.

The next year, on Wednesday morning, the thirteenth of April, ice fell and the white vines withered in it.

When Mu'āwiya became king, as he wanted, and had a respite from civil wars, he broke the truce with the Romans and no longer accepted a truce from them. Rather, he said, "If the Romans seek a truce, let them give up their weapons and pay the tax."

[folio missing in the manuscript]

... of the year. Yazīd son of Mu'āwiya again went up with a powerful army. When they camped at Thrace, the Arabs dispersed for plunder, [leaving] their hirelings and young men for the shepherding of livestock and for any sort of spoils that might befall them. When those standing on the wall [saw this], they fell upon them, [killed] many of the young men and hirelings, as well as some of the Arab [men], carried off the plunder, and [re-] entered [the city].

The next day, all the young men of the city assembled, along with some of those who had entered there to take refuge, as well as a few Romans. They said, "Let us go out against them." Constantine said to them, "Do not go forth. For you have not waged a war and been victorious. Rather, you [just] stole." They did not listen to him. Instead, having armed themselves, many people went out. In accord with Roman custom, they raised standards and banners. As soon as they went out, all the porticoes were closed and the king set up his tent on the wall, sat, and watched. The Saracens drew back and retreated far from the wall so that when [their opponents] should flee, they could not quickly escape. They stationed themselves by tribe. When [their opponents] reached them, [the Saracens] leaped up and cried out in their language, "God is great." And immediately they fled. The Saracens ran after them until they reached [the range] of the walls' ballistae, devastating them and taking captives. Constantine was angry with them and

73

wanted to refuse to open [the porticoes] for them. Many of them fell, and others were wounded by arrows.

In the year 975 [663/64 C.E.], the twenty-second of Constans and the seventh of Mu'āwiya, Bar Khālid, the general of the Arabs of Emesa, the capital of Phoenicia, went up and led an army against Roman territory. He made camp by a lake called 'Sqdryn. When he saw that many people inhabited [the middle] of it, he tried to conquer it. He made rafts and boats, sailed the army on them, and sent [the army] to the middle [of the lake]. When those in the middle [of the lake] saw [the Arabs], they fled and hid from them. When the Arabs reached the dry land in the middle [of the lake], they disembarked, tied up their boats, and prepared to attack the people. Immediately, those who had been hiding rose up, ran, cut the boats' ropes, and steered them into the deep. The Arabs were left in the harbor, on land surrounded by deep water and mud. The [inhabitants] of the middle [of the lake] assembled, surrounded them from all sides, fell upon them with slings, rocks, and arrows, and killed all of them. [The Arabs'] comrades standing on the opposite [shore] saw [what was happening] but were unable to help them. Until this day, the Arabs have not again attacked this lake.

Bar Khālid departed from there and gave a guarantee to the city of Amorium. When they opened [the city] to him, he installed a garrison of Arabs there. He departed from there and went against the great fortress of Sylws, because a master carpenter from the region of Paphlagonia had tricked him and said to him, "If you give me and my household a guarantee [of safety], I will make you a catapult that will capture this fortress." Bar Khālid gave him [the guarantee] and issued a command. They brought long planks, and [the carpenter] made a catapult the like of which they had never seen. They went up and set up [the catapult] opposite the fortress's portico. Because they trusted its 74 strength, the fortress's masters allowed them to approach the fortress. When Khālid's men shot their catapult, a rock flew up and struck the fortress's gate. Next they threw another rock, but it fell a little short. Again, they threw a third rock, but it fell short of the previous ones. Those above cried out derisively, saying, "Khālid's men, shoot [harder], for you are shooting badly." And immediately with [their] catapult they threw down a large stone. It fell and struck Bar Khālid's catapult, destroyed it, and [then] rolled downhill and killed many people.

Bar Khālid went from there and conquered the fortresses of *Psynws, Kyws,* and Pergamum, as well as the city of Smyrna.

Syriac Life of Maximus
the Confessor

Maronite

Possibly late seventh century C.E.

The document whose Syriac title reads "The history of the wicked Maximus of Palestine, who blasphemed against his creator and whose tongue was torn out" is generally known to modern scholars by the less colorful name *Syriac Life of Maximus the Confessor.* Maximus the Confessor (d. 662) was a key opponent of the mid-seventh-century doctrine of Monotheletism, the belief that, although Christ has a divine nature and a human nature, he has a single will. Initially championed by the Byzantine emperor Heraclius as a compromise solution to the Christological controversies, Monotheletism quickly became a new source of contention. Maximus's opposition to Monotheletism eventually resulted in his mutilation and exile. Nevertheless, his views ultimately won the day, and in the early 680s the Sixth Ecumenical Council officially condemned Monotheletism. But by that point the controversy had already resulted in a schism among

Chalcedonian Christians. In particular, even after the Sixth Ecumenical Council, a group originally associated with the monastery of Maron (hence known as Maronites) continued to support Monotheletism, even though in later centuries the Maronites eventually disavowed this doctrine.

The *Syriac Life of Maximus the Confessor* was born out of this theological controversy. Written from a Maronite, pro-Mono-thelete perspective, this polemical "tell-all" of the most famous opponent of Monotheletism begins with Maximus's birth from the illegitimate union of a Samaritan and a Persian slave owned by a Jew. According to the narrator, Maximus was later orphaned and taken in by a blasphemous follower of the mid-third-century "heretic" Origen. As he matured, Maximus propagated heretical teachings until he was anathematized by the Byzantine emperor Heraclius. This temporarily restored the church's theological unity and forced Maximus into hiding.

At this point the *Life* first mentions the Arabs (and it is here where the following translation begins). Throughout the remainder of the extant document, the spread of Maximus's teaching has a direct correlation with the spread of Arab rule. According to the narrator, Maximus's success is both cause and consequence of Arab military expansion. On the one hand, the conquests created enough unrest to prevent an effective ecclesiastical response to Maximus's heresy. On the other hand, Arab military success could also be seen as punishment of those Christians who had accepted Maximus's theology. Thus the second half of the story is essentially a travelogue tracing the alleged movements of Maximus and his right-hand man, Anastasios, as well as Arab forces.

This story, in which the Arabs serve as the catalyst and the punishment of Christian heresy, not only preserves a Maronite interpretation of the Islamic conquests. Its frequent allusions to Arab troop movements and temporary truces between Byzantine and Arab rulers also provide useful data for better understanding the military and political history of the mid-seventh century. The document's polemical nature requires that these references not be accepted uncritically. Nevertheless, there is little doubt that the *Syriac Life of Maximus the Confessor* contains some important kernels of historical realia.

MANUSCRIPT AND EDITION

The *Syriac Life of Maximus the Confessor* appears in a unique, fragmentary manuscript now housed in the British Library. As currently bound, *British Library Additional* 7192 contains two manuscripts. The first fifty folios come from a most likely seventh-century manuscript containing a polemical work by Peter of Kallinikos. The last twenty-eight folios come from a separate, incomplete manuscript that Sebastian Brock and William Wright have dated on paleographic grounds to the seventh or eighth century. This manuscript begins with excerpts from two earlier texts, the *Julian Romance* and an astronomic tractate ascribed to Dionysius the Areopagite. The surviving pages end with four brief documents opposing Maximus the Confessor: a censuring of the Sixth Council, which opposed Monotheletism, two texts posing questions to the "Maximianists," and the last document extant in the manuscript, the *Syriac Life of Maximus the Confessor.* Unfortunately, the surviving manuscript pages break off before the *Syriac Life* has concluded.

The manuscript's transmission also reflects ongoing theological tensions. A later reader slightly modified the *Life*'s title, erasing the words *wicked* and *blasphemed* from the text's initial characterization of Maximus. It is unclear if this change occurred because the manuscript moved from a Maronite to a non-Maronite community or because of the Maronites' changing views of Monotheletism. In either case, this later reader, despite partially rehabilitating Maximus's legacy, left the rest of the text's anti-Maximus polemic unmodified. Brock published an edition of the *Life* in 1973.

AUTHORSHIP AND DATE OF COMPOSITION

The narrator claims to be George of Resh'aina, an otherwise unknown figure. He states that he was a bishop under Sophronios, the Chalcedonian patriarch of Jerusalem (d. 638). Brock has tried to substantiate this assertion. He points to a Syriac manuscript containing a set of mid-seventh-century Monothelete quotations also attributed to a bishop named George. Brock then suggests that both George Resh'aina, the purported author of the pro-Monothelete *Syriac Life of Maximus the Confessor,* and George the mid-seventh-century author of these pro-Monothelete fragments are the same person. If he is correct and these two Georges are one and the same, this would help substantiate the text's authorial claim and point toward a mid- to late seventh-century composition date. On the other hand, there remains a strong possibility that the text is pseudonymous. In that case, determining the date before which it must have been written would rely on Wright's and Brock's paleographic judgment concerning the only surviving manuscript. If accurate, this would still place the text's composition in a seventh- or eighth-century context.

· · ·

Next, the history of the wicked Maximus of Palestine, who blasphemed against his creator and whose tongue was torn out . . .

… While, along with Maximus's student Sergios, his pupil Anastasios was serving him, Maximus confined himself to a small cell out of fear of the emperor and those patriarchs who had anathematized his teaching. He stayed in this cell until the Arabs appeared and took control of Syrian and many [other] places.

Heresy is accustomed to running alongside paganism and for its sustenance to gain strength from a sent chastisement. So when this wretch saw that the land had become the Arabs' and that there no longer was anyone to hinder and abolish his doctrine, he once again publically professed his deception and began sowing his teaching among some in the regions of Syria. Since the victorious Emperor Heraclius, his son Constantine, as well as Heraklonas and his mother had [all] died, Constantine's son Constans received the Romans' kingdom while a little child. [Because of this] and also because at that time Africa was again rebelling against the emperor, Maximus grew eager and immediately took Anastasios and the other brethren with him, departed, and entered Africa.

Anastasios was [well] known in the region because, as we had previously said, he had been born there. They went and entered a monastery at the upper tip of Africa that in Latin is called Hippo Diarrhytos. Some students from Nisibis were dwelling there. The monastery's abbot was Isaiah, and his son called Jesus [was also there]. They were about eighty-seven monks and were Nestorians. When they found that in their teachings Maximus and Anastasios agreed with the teaching of their master Nestorius, they accepted them, agreed with their doctrine, and led all Africa astray. None in Africa disputed them except for a God-loving hermit named Luke, by whom they were defeated through God's power. And [Luke] immediately sent [word]

310

311

about them to Constantinople (indeed, it was for this very hermit that the pious Makarios, the patriarch of Antioch, produced
three books against Maximus's doctrine).

They sowed their weeds and led astray everyone they could
in Africa, so that they even led astray the prefect there, named
George. Afterward, fear of the Arabs compelled them to depart
from there, and they entered Sicily. For through [the Arabs']
deeds, God's wrath overtook the entire region of Africa. After
they went about all the ocean islands, they even went up to
Rome.

Through the guile of their deceit, even Martin the patriarch
there was deceived. He accepted [Maximus's] entire doctrine.
So he assembled a synod of 190 bishops that affirmed Maximus's
confession and anathematized the patriarchs of Constantinople
because they were unwilling to agree with him.) Therefore,
Emperor Constans became angry with him, summoned him,
and took him to the capital city. He demanded that [Martin]
turn away from the evil of his doctrine. But when [Martin] was
not persuaded, [Constans] sent him into exile, to Lazika, in the
days when the pious Pyrrhus was the patriarch of that city and
Macedonius was [the patriarch] of Antioch. There [Martin]
died an evil death. For not through Constans's command had he
become patriarch; rather [Martin] had come to Constantinople
through fraudulent documents that he had forged and through
the contrivance of a clever patrician called Theodoros.

And when he went to the holy city of Jerusalem to pray during a truce between Emperor Constans and Mu'āwiya, the emir
of the Arabs, 'Rmg[.]bwlqr', who had succeeded Emperor Heraclius's brother Theodoros, told me all the other things that I am
going to write concerning Maximus, Anastasios, and those
monks who because of the Arabs fled Africa and went up to

312

Rome to this Martin, whom I spoke about. For I took great care to write this story truthfully.

After Maximus went up to Rome, the Arabs took control of the ocean's islands. They entered Cyprus and Arwad, destroyed them, and took [their inhabitants] captive. They took control of Africa and conquered almost all of the ocean's islands. Following the wicked Maximus, God's wrath punished everywhere that had accepted his error.

Those students who were in the monastery of Hippo Diarrhytos (which we had previously spoken of) fled before the Arabs and went up to Rome. Martin accepted them as fellow believers and gave them a monastery that in Latin is called *Cellae novaes* (which is translated as "Nine cells"). They remained in their error, leading astray everyone they could.

When Maximus saw that Rome had accepted the rotting filth of his blasphemies, he also went down to Constantinople in the time when Mu'āwiya had made a truce with Emperor Constans while he fought a war with Abū Turāb, the emir of Ḥirta, at Ṣiffīn and defeated him and Emperor Constans was in Azerbaijan. At that time, Maximus entered Constantinople hoping that he might also devastate it through his error, as [he had] the other [cities].

Maximus immediately entered and stayed at a woman's convent in the city called Plakidias. Through his maliciousness, he was able to lead them astray from truth and ... them to his wicked faith. He ... in the Eucharist ...

Canons

GEORGE I

East Syrian

676 C.E.

George I served as the head, the catholicos, of the East Syrians from 660/61 to 680/81. In 676 he convened a synod on the island of Diren (modern-day Bahrain) in the Persian Gulf. The synod produced a document consisting of a preface followed by nineteen canons. Although it addresses a variety of issues, several parts of this document are particularly relevant as early Christian reactions to Islam.

The preface includes one of the earliest extant references to the traditional Muslim calendar and states that the synod was convened during the fifty-seventh year of the Arabs' rule. A handful of late seventh-century Syriac manuscripts also uses hijra dating. However, unlike this synod's document, all of them include not only a hijra date but also the more common Seleucid dating system that Syriac Christians had been using for centuries. The preface is also important because of its interest in law and legal traditions. Although earlier Syriac documents also speak of jurisprudence, this topic was increasingly pressing with the rise of Islam and its insistence that non-Muslims in the Islamic Empire either have their own robust system of civil law or become subject to Islamic law. Several modern scholars have suggested that this preface's focus on the necessity of law is a direct reaction to this postconquest legal environment.

Three of the synod's nineteen canons may also have been composed in response to Islam. Canon Six addresses an issue that was increasingly prominent in postconquest Syriac canon law, the concern of Christians seeking more favorable rulings in nonecclesiastical courts. The canon speaks generically against Christians bringing legal matters "outside the church" and of "secular rulers." Nevertheless, given the historical context, it is almost certain that many of these rulers would have been Muslims. Canon Fourteen speaks against women who dwell and unite with "pagans." The Syriac word (*ḥanpē*) here translated as "pagans" is the traditional term of Syriac authors for polytheists. But after the conquests, some Syriac authors also used it to speak of Muslims. As a result, this canon may also have been written with Muslims in mind and—at the very least—was interpreted this way by later readers. Additionally, the word (*'ṯḥalaṭ*) translated as "unite with" can also have the meaning of "marry." Combined with the word (*'mar*) for "to dwell," this suggests that George and his bishops were also concerned about issues of intermarriage. Canon Nineteen is the most explicit of the synod's references to Islamic rule and forbids the laity from collecting the poll tax (in Syriac, *ksep rishā;* in Arabic, *jizya*) from bishops.

Late Umayyad- and early Abbasid-era Syriac texts address in greater detail each of these issues: hijra dating, the systematizing of Christian jurisprudence, prohibitions on Christians going to nonecclesiastical courts, concerns of interreligious mingling, intermarriage, and forbidding the laity from collecting the poll tax from clergy. The canons from George I are particularly important, as they document the earliest reactions to such concerns.

MANUSCRIPTS AND EDITION

The synod's rulings are preserved in four manuscripts written between the fourteenth and twentieth centuries. Two are now housed in the Vatican Library, one in the Bibliothèque Nationale in Paris, and one in Baghdad. Another was kept in Siirt in Turkey but most likely was destroyed after World War I. In 1902 Jean-Baptiste Chabot published an edition based on the Vatican manuscript *Borgia Syriac* 82, which was copied in 1869 from a most likely fourteenth-century exemplar.

AUTHORSHIP AND DATE OF COMPOSITION

George I was born into a noble family in northern Iraq and attended the famous East Syrian monastery of Bēt ʿAbē. The catholicos Ishoʿyahb III appointed him the metropolitan bishop of Abiabene. Upon Ishoʿyahb's death, circa 660, George became the catholicos and served as the head of the East Syrian church until his death in 680 or 681. The synod's preface states that the bishops convened in "May of the year 57 of the Arabs' rule." Assuming the bishops correctly calculated the hijra date, the synod took place in 676 C.E.

•   •   •

Next, the synod of our holy and blessed father Mār George—blessed catholicos patriarch—and of the pious fathers who arrived and gathered in the region of Qaṭrayē.

Our good, all-wise God simultaneously assigned the human race temporal life and a mortal body. He gave the weakness of mortality dominion over them always so that, through persistent labor, those accustomed to the fear of God might procure for themselves profit for their souls. Virtue and love of God have been naturally implanted in us by our wise creator. Nevertheless, on account of the soul's inclination and the body's enticements, many in this life [have fallen] under the error of forgetfulness. Therefore, the exalted care of our most venerated God did not leave us without the aid and support of laws, written by the spirit, that raise the mind to the true good.

In every generation and every people, he assigned moderate laws suitable for the times and [the people] of those times so that the benefit of his aid would not perish from the mind's memory, through error and through wandering after the many things that cause one to stray from the fear of God. At first, for the benefit of the descendants of Adam, Noah, and Abraham, and up to Moses, the omnipotent Lord threateningly put [his] warnings in the imperative and led [them] toward the fear of his name. Afterward, through Moses's fingers, he established a book of various laws for the ancient people that is the shadow of the mystery of the New [Testament]. Afterward, through the glorious dawning of his beloved—who, like the sun, shines over the whole world—he handed the gospel of salvation over to his church. For through the life-giving laws that cast [one] from earth and lead [one] to heaven, [the church] might be guided to the straight, holy paths until it receives the exalted promises of life cast from death, which have neither weakness nor deviation, nor need of such laws and commandments.

Thus the holy apostles, as well as the priests and teachers after them, established laws according to [their] time, necessity, and need, and they taught men to journey on the path of righteousness. Therefore, the helpful laws accumulated and greatly multiplied throughout the entire church, in the West and in the East. For [laws] were established and written in their times by   216
the holy, pious fathers, [laws] whose use gave humankind endless assistance.

But in every age, the variety and multitude of humanity's weaknesses (in accordance with the affairs occurring among every nation and place, those [affairs] that [each] age renews in its difficulty) necessitate that those designated by God's grace for the governance of their souls diligently help [the soul's] correction, both orally and through written precepts that for prolonged times are necessary to increase the mind's memory. Therefore, it pleased our Lord's mercy that, on our visit, we to whom befalls the lot of ecclesiastical governance in this difficult age of the world's end would be taken to the ocean islands placed in the south of the world to complete the ministry of [the islands'] inhabitants. [Here] we found certain things that needed to be renewed for those Christ-loving people, through the establishment of correct laws that keep [those who] fulfill them within the boundaries of the fear of God.

In this month of May of the year 57 of the Arabs' rule, after visiting the islands and other places, we reached the holy church on the island of Diren. We who were there were

I, George, who by God's grace am catholicos, patriarch of the East

I, Thomas, who by grace am the metropolitan bishop of Bēt Qaṭrayē

I, Ishoʿyahb, who by grace am the bishop of the island of Diren

I, Sergius, who by grace am the bishop of Ṭrihan

I, Stephen, who by grace am the bishop of Mazunyē

I, Pousai, who by grace am the bishop of Hagar

I, Souhai, who by grace am the bishop of Haṭṭā

When we took care of all the things needing correction, there was found among them some remaining things that especially needed their correction committed to writing in written canons. For, even if among them were things that had been previously established by our holy fathers in prior councils, nevertheless necessity required that their memory be renewed by us in this book.

Thus we begin by the power of the Holy Spirit, with the consent of all of us, to establish these matters and to write down their reform as an aid to the inhabitants of these places.

[Canon] Six. *Concerning the lawsuits of Christians: that they should take place in [the] church before those designated by the bishop with the community's consent, [namely] priests and [other] believers, and that those who are to be judged should not go outside the church and [be judged] before pagans or [other] unbelievers.* Lawsuits and disputes between Christians should be judged in the church. And [the litigants] should not go outside [the church] like those without law. They should be judged before judges who have been designated by the bishop with the community's consent, priests who are known for 220 [their] love of truth and fear of God and who possess knowledge and competency in [such] affairs. They should not [do] otherwise and, on account of the [litigants'] vehemence of their opinion, take their affairs outside the church. But if there is something that has been concealed from those who have been appointed for the judgment of lawsuits, [the litigants] should bring their petition before the bishop, and from him they will receive an answer regarding what disturbs them. For, in accord with our Lord's word, none of the believers is permitted to take up the judgment of believers' lawsuits on his own authority without the bishop's command and the community's consent, unless necessity arises [through] the commandment of secular rulers.

[Canon] Fourteen. *Concerning that Christian women should not unite with pagans, [who are] strangers to the fear of God.* Women who once believed in Christ and want to live a Christian life, with all their might let them avoid uniting with pagans, as uniting with them they accustom themselves to practices that are foreign to the fear of God and they acquire a weak will. Therefore, Christian women should completely abstain from dwelling with pagans. And, in accord with our Lord's word, let any woman who dares [to do] this be far from the church and from all Christian honor.

224

[Canon] Nineteen. *Concerning the bishop and his due honor and that those believers placed in authority are not allowed to demand tribute from him.* The honor of the bishop who beautifully fulfills his ministry and is upright in his service—let him be distinguished from his flock by all suitable things that he might be honored and pleased by them. For those believers holding authority are not permitted to demand the poll tax and tribute from him as from laity. For [bishops] bear the honor of their rule in the fulfillment of its ministry, and, in accord with the pastoral law, [honor]

keeps vigil over them and endures their difficulties. Therefore,
226   on account on this, [believers] are obliged to honor [the bishop]
and not demand the poll tax from him as [they do] from other
men. But if they dare [to do] this, let them know that they are
condemned by righteousness....

Colophon of *British Library Additional* 14,666

East Syrian
682 C.E.

British Library Additional 14,666, f. 56, is the only surviving leaf of a no longer extant New Testament manuscript written in 682. This page originally contained the last twenty-seven verses of a Syriac translation of Hebrews, as well as the codex's colophon, a concluding scribal note. Unfortunately, even these fragments are only partially preserved. Nevertheless, the colophon's surviving text includes most of the dating formula, which speaks of the reckoning "of the Hagarenes, the sons of Ishmael." The colophon is one of the earliest examples of Syriac use of a hijra date and properly correlates A.G. 993 in the Seleucid dating system most commonly used by Syriac Christians (681–82 C.E.) with A.H. 63 in the hijra dating system (682–83 C.E.). Its vocabulary is also significant, including one of the earliest uses of "Hagarene" (*mhaggrāyē*), a term it puts in apposition with "sons of Ishmael."

MANUSCRIPT AND EDITION

The shelf mark of *British Library Additional* 14,666 does not refer to a single manuscript. Instead, it designates a diverse collection of manuscript fragments that, in the mid-nineteenth century, were bound into a single volume. In 1870 William Wright published an edition of the surviving colophon.

AUTHORSHIP AND DATE OF COMPOSITION

After the dating formula, the colophon is only fragmentarily preserved and no longer includes the scribe's name. Nevertheless, the surviving list of ecclesiastical officials indicates that it was composed by an East Syrian scribe. The years A.G. 993 and A.H. 63 overlapped for only three weeks in September. If the scribe had his dates right, the codex was completed sometime between September 10 and 30, 682 C.E.

. . .

This book of the New [Testament] was completed in the year 993 according to [the reckoning] of the Greeks, which is the year 63 according to that of the Hagarenes, the sons of Ish[mael], the son of Hagar and Abraham.

Letter

ATHANASIUS OF BALAD

Miaphysite

684 C.E.

Early in his life, Athanasius of Balad studied at the Miaphysite monastery of Qenneshrē, a renowned center of Greek learning. Having become an avid translator of Greek, he also became famous as a biblical interpreter. In 684 C.E. Athanasius was elected the Miaphysite patriarch. He died in 687. Although later chronicles briefly speak of his patriarchate, only one of his writings survives from these last three years of his life, an encyclical addressing the issue of Christians mingling with ḥanpē.

In this letter, Athanasius instructs rural bishops (*chorespiscopi*) and ecclesiastical visitors (*periodeuta*) to better regulate interactions between Christians and ḥanpē. He is particularly concerned about Christians who eat of non-Christian sacrifices. He also mentions the marrying of Christian women and ḥanpē men. Although the Syriac term Athanasius uses here, *zwg,* can simply mean "to mix with or mingle," it also often means "to marry."

79

Later in the letter, it becomes clear that he is indeed concerned about issues of intermarriage, as he refers to the children that stem from these unions. Unlike many other authors, however, Athanasius stresses that an intermarried Christian woman may still receive the Eucharist. He ends his letter by briefly addressing two other ritual regulations: baptism and the Eucharist should not be given to those Christians whom he considers heretical, including a branch of Miaphysites called Julianists; and, most likely because candidates were baptized naked, men and women should be baptized separately. Earlier documents, such as the third-century church order called the *Didascalia*, also addressed this issue and specified that deaconesses should assist in the baptism of female initiates. Athanasius may be alluding to a similar procedure.

With the exception of the last few sentences, the letter focuses on the interactions of Christians and *ḥanpē*, making this word key to understanding Athanasius's missive. Most typically, this Syriac word refers to pagans, and it remains quite likely that this is exactly how Athanasius used it as well. Such a usage would make the best sense of his repeated references to the *ḥanpē*'s sacrifices, as pagan sacrifices had been the target of Christian invective since the first century. Indeed, the letter's reference to the "food of their sacrifices and to what is strangled" alludes to Acts 15:20, 15:29, and 21:25, which speak of what polytheists have sacrificed to idols. Although it remains possible that Athanasius wanted the term *ḥanpē* to be read on more than one level, given its primary meaning of "pagan" that is the translation I use in the following letter.

Nevertheless, two developments made this letter significant for Christian-Muslim relations as well. First, although Syriac authors continued to use *ḥanpē* to speak of polytheists, in the decades following Athanasius's letter this term was increasingly used as a polemical way to refer to Muslims. Thus, for later readers, the object of Athanasius's invective became unclear. Had the patriarch written against Christians mingling with polytheists or with Muslims? In other words, because of the changing meaning of *ḥanpē*, Athanasius's letter could easily be read as a prohibition against certain Christian-Muslim interactions. Second, most likely in the eighth century, a Miaphysite scribe removed any ambiguity by adding a title to the letter that summarizes it as "A letter from the blessed Patriarch Athanasius concerning this: that a Christian may not eat from the sacrifices of those Hagarenes who now rule." It is possible that upon finding the term *ḥanpē* in this letter, whoever wrote the later title sincerely believed that Athanasius had been writing against Muslims. Alternatively, the scribe may have seen an easy opportunity to redirect the now dead patriarch's authority against Islam. In either case, instead of using Athanasius's term *ḥanpē*, this later scribe referred to Hagarenes, a term used exclusively for Muslims. Just to be safe, he even specified "the Hagarenes who now rule." This combination of later Syriac Christians using *ḥanpē* as a polemical way to connote Muslims and the letter's new title effectively transformed the patriarch's encyclical into an anti-Muslim tractate.

MANUSCRIPTS AND EDITIONS

Nine known manuscripts preserve Athanasius's letter. Three of these were copied in the centuries immediately following his death. On paleographic grounds, *Mardin* 310 and *Vatican Syriac* 560 have been dated to the eighth century and *Paris Syriac* 62 to the ninth. The remainder are much more recent. *Vatican Borg.*

Syriac 148 was written in 1576, *Sarf. Patr.* 87 in 1907, *Sarf. Patr.* 73 in 1911, *Birmingham Mingana Syriac* 8 in 1911, and *Mardin* 322 and *Mardin* 337 most likely in the early twentieth century. In these manuscripts, Athanasius's letter most often appears among other documents concerning canon law. In 1909 François Nau produced an edition of Athanasius's letter based on *Paris Syriac* 62. In 2013 Rifaat Ebied published an edition based on *Birmingham Mingana Syriac* 8.

AUTHORSHIP AND DATE OF COMPOSITION

Athanasius was the Miaphysite patriarch from 684 to 687. Most manuscripts include a marginal note attributing this letter to 684. Modern scholars agree that the letter's current title, which specifies that Athanasius was writing against Christians eating the sacrifices of Hagarenes, was not original to this work but was added later. Nevertheless, this incipit appears in the earliest manuscripts, suggesting that the current title had become an integral part of the work by the eighth century at least. As a result, a Miaphysite scribe seems to have successfully repackaged what was most likely originally an antipagan polemic and redeployed it against Muslims.

·   ·   ·

Next, a letter from the blessed Patriarch Athanasius concerning this: that a Christian may not eat from the sacrifices of those Hagarenes who now rule.

To the excellent and God-loving spiritual children, to the beloved rural bishops and the faithful visitors everywhere. The lowly Athanasius greets [you] in the Lord.

Moved by forgiveness, affection, and fatherly love toward all the faithful children of God's holy church, [as best as] our lowly power is able, we take proper care and caution concerning their progress and salvation. Although we are not worthy [to be] one to whom God has entrusted the position and office of a watchman, we do fear God's threat and judgment were we to refrain from sounding a trumpet and warning his people, as we have been commanded. We have composed this epistle of exhortation on your love of God so that through your intervention and zeal you might cut off the evil and sin of this wickedness that we have heard is now in God's church.

For an evil report has come to the hearing of our lowliness that some accursed Christians—that is, greedy men who are slaves to the belly—at meals heedlessly and senselessly mingle together with pagans. Also, wretched women in some manner or another unlawfully and inappropriately marry pagan men. Sometimes all of them eat without distinction from their sacrifices. In their negligence, they forget those apostolic commands and admonitions concerning this that [so] often cry out to those believing in Christ [saying] that they should abstain from fornication, from what is strangled, from blood, and from meals of pagan sacrifices lest they become partners with demons and their abominable table.

But your discernment will be mindful [of this]. Inflamed—as is your custom—with knowledge and divine zeal you will rise up. With all your power, you will stop, abolish, and cause to be entirely forgotten this evil and destructive laxity among all your fellow Christians summoned by the Lord's name. Those whom you carefully learn are negligently being besmeared by sin such as this, from now on instruct them in the precepts and ecclesiastical canons. For you know that they command concerning things such as this. And, in accord with the wise and cautious distinction [mandated by] the commandments of the

129

Holy Spirit, prevent them from participating in the divine mysteries while you intelligently deal with them according to each one's intention, knowledge, and power.

Exhort, admonish, and warn the rest—particularly those women who in this fashion marry those [pagans]—to keep themselves from the food of sacrifices, from what is strangled, and from all unlawful mingling. With all their might let them also take care to baptize their children who come from their union with them. If you find them to behave in every way worthy of a Christian, do not cut them off from participation in the divine mysteries solely because they openly and freely marry pagans.

And concerning this: that no orthodox priest should knowingly and willingly give holy baptism or participation in the divine mysteries to Nestorians, Julianists, or any other of the heretics. We judge sufficient that decree which through anathemas we and our pious fellow bishops of the East issued against any priest or deacon who dares to do something like this. It also generally pleases all of us that males do not receive females from baptism and also females do not [receive] males. Due to caution and lest the Christian mysteries be dishonored, indeed [they should not receive] each other. [This letter] is finished.

Book of Main Points

JOHN BAR PENKĀYĒ

East Syrian

ca. 687 C.E.

In the late 680s, the abbot of the East Syrian monastery of John Kāmul asked one of his monks, John of Fenek (more commonly known as John bar Penkāyē), to write a theological response to contemporary events. John evidently took his abbot's request quite seriously, as it motivated him to write more than four hundred pages of text. Titled *Book of Main Points,* the resulting narrative traces the world's history from creation until the late 680s.

John wrote during the second Arab civil war, which began soon after the death of the caliph Muʻāwiya II in 683. For the following nine years, the Umayyad caliphs Marwān (r. 684–85) and his son ʻAbd al-Malik (r. 685–705) fought against a rival caliph, ʻAbd Allah ibn al-Zubayr (d. 692). To make John's situation more precarious, when he composed the *Book of Main Points,* his region of Iraq was not under the control of any of these contending caliphs. Rather, a group of non-Arab prisoners of war had staged an initially successful anti-Arab rebellion and had recently taken the city of Nisibis, a hundred kilometers southwest of John's monastery. During this time of local rebellion amid a much larger civil war, John wrote his fifteen-book world history.

The question of theodicy dominates the work. How could a just God allow late seventh-century Christians to suffer as they did? John's answer drew on paradigms that the church historian Eusebius of Caesarea (d. ca. 339) had popularized, as well as an extensive East Syrian tradition of understanding God's dealings with humanity in terms of divine pedagogy. He then interpreted the previous six centuries of church history as a cycle of Christians learning from their tribulations, growing closer to God, and—once their situation improved—falling back into error. Applying this heuristic to the contemporary situation, the *Book of Main Points* claims that once Roman persecution of Christians subsided in the early fourth century, theological error overtook the church. The resulting Chalcedonian theology led to the Byzantines' defeat by the Arabs. As for the Persians, they were defeated because of their excessive pride and because of Zoroastrian persecution of East Syrian Christians.

What would happen next? John here diverges from earlier seventh-century Syriac authors. According to him, humanity had already missed its last chance for reform. Realizing that nothing would motivate humanity to repent, God had removed his heavenly care from the world, ushering in the beginning of the end. As for the Sons of Hagar, according to John, they would soon be defeated by the anti-Arab forces that had recently taken control of Nisibis, a group whom he calls *Shurṭē*. Their victory, however, would also be short-lived, as John knows "that the end of ages has reached us."

Although John dedicated only one full book of his world history to discussing the Sons of Hagar, the *Book of Main Points* represents a quintessential example of remembering the past through the lens of the present. Due to the tribulations that he and his community faced during the second Arab civil war, John was convinced that the world would soon end. This motivated him to look back in time to establish an ongoing pattern of God's pedagogical relationship with humanity and to find the decisive moment, the conquests and their immediate aftermath, when this pattern was broken beyond repair.

The *Book of Main Points* presents an elaborate East Syrian theological response to the Islamic conquests. Although John bar Penkāyē had a very specific agenda, because he was an eye-witness to many of the events he describes, his work remains a particularly important historical source for understanding the rise of Islam, especially the political and military events of the 680s. His narrative also documents the rise of Christian apocalyptic expectations that characterize many late seventh-century Syriac writings.

MANUSCRIPTS AND EDITION

The *Book of Main Points* appears in more than a dozen extant manuscripts, the oldest of which is dated 1874/75. The remainder are from the later nineteenth and early twentieth centuries. Fortunately, the 1874/75 manuscript includes a colophon stating that its scribe copied the text from an exemplar dating from 1262. As a result, at least some of the surviving manuscripts most likely preserve a version of the *Book of Main Points* that stems from at least the thirteenth century. No one has yet made a critical edition. In 1907 Alphonse Mingana produced the only published edition of John's work, but he included only books 10–15, based primarily on the earliest extant manuscript, *Mosul 26.*

AUTHORSHIP AND DATE OF COMPOSITION

John was born in northwest Mesopotamia in the town of Fenek. When he wrote the *Book of Main Points,* he was a monk at the East Syrian monastery of John Kāmul under the abbot Sabrisho'. According to medieval Syriac authors, at some point he moved to the Monastery of Mār Bassaimā. No one has contested John's authorship of this work.

The last securely dated event in the text is the death of the rebel leader Mukhtār, which Muslim sources assign to April 3, 687. John's belief that the *Shurṭē* would ultimately defeat the Arabs points toward his writing this work prior to 690, when these rebels were defeated. His narrative also seems to assume that 'Abd Allah ibn al-Zubayr was still contending for the caliphate. Similarly, John mentions the East Syrian catholicos as being Ḥnanisho' I, whose reign ended in 692/93. Taken together, these historical references strongly suggest that he wrote his *Book of Main Points* in 687 or very soon afterward.

·   ·   ·

In the days of their king Khosrau, when the kingdom of the Persians came to an end, the kingdom of the Sons of Hagar immediately spread over more or less the entire world. For they seized the entire kingdom of the Persians, and they overthrew all their warriors, who had been exceedingly proud in the arts of war. Indeed, we should not consider their coming to be ordinary. For it was a divine deed. Prior to summoning them, [God] had previously prepared them to hold Christians in honor. Thus there also carefully came from God a certain commandment that they should hold our monastic order in honor. And when they came in accord with a divine commandment, they seized—so to say—the two kingdoms without war or difficulty. With neither armor nor human wiles, in a despised fashion, like a brand snatched from a fire, God gave victory into their hands so that what was written concerning them could be fulfilled: "One pursued a thousand, and two put ten thousand to flight" [Dt 32:30]. For, apart from divine aid, how could naked men riding with neither armor nor shield be victorious? He summoned them from the ends of the earth to devastate a sinful kingdom and with them to humble the arrogance of the Sons of Persia.

Only a little time passed, and the entire land was handed over to the Arabs. They conquered all the fortified cities, and they ruled from ocean to ocean, from east to west, Egypt and all of Methrain, and from Crete to Cappadocia, from Yāhelmān to the gates of Elān—Armenians, Syrians, Persians, Romans, Egyptians—and all the regions in between. [It was] in accord with the prophet's word, "their hand was over all" [Gn 16:12]. Except for half of the Romans' kingdom, [nothing] remained from them. Who can relate the slaughter they made in the Greek Empire, in Kush, in Spain, and in the rest of the distant regions, taking their sons and daughters captive and reducing them to slaves. Upon those who in peace and prosperity ceaselessly battled with their creator there was sent a barbaric people who showed them no pity. But because we have reached this point in the account, let us here end this book and offer praise to the Father, Son, and Holy Spirit forever. Amen.

The End of Book Fourteen

Book Fifteen

For while our affairs were thus progressing through divine care and without human assistance, through the power of the victorious king we appeared glorious against all battles brought upon us by tyrannical kings. As long as pagan kings ruled, all our ranks were properly conducted because, on account of fear of persecutors, the lax and dissolute were not allowed to remain among us. As soon as someone [drifting] from vigilance of the truth fell asleep, the furnace of persecution would separate him [from us] without the bother of a council. But from time to time, when the vehemence of our persecution lessened a little, in accord with tradition, the fathers would assemble, judge a few accusations that had sprung up, dispel perplexities that had arisen, affirm the apostolic cannons, and [do] other appropriate things that the age had taught them to set right and to establish.

144   Therefore, as I said, our faith flourished greatly and our conduct was radiant. For even though there were many councils before that of Nicaea, they were neither universal nor to make a new creed. Rather, [they took place] for the purpose that we spoke of above. But after there was relief and believing kings took control of the Roman government, then corruption and perplexity entered the churches. Creeds and councils multiplied because every year they made a new creed. Rest and peace brought them great loss. For lovers of glory did not stop stirring up trouble. Rather, they stole the obedience of kings with gold and played with them like children. These were the things concerning the Romans.

Now, because until the coming of the Sons of Hagar the church of the Persian Empire had been put under Magian [i.e., Zoroastrian] rule, it had nothing else to battle against. Although some offenses sprung up, they were not allowed to flourish. For before [they flourished], our Lord suppressed them. While these things progressed like this from the apostles' time until the kingdom of this last Khosrau, our savior, who foresees everything before it takes place, saw how great a cause of loss much rest would be for us. [He saw] the evil things toward which we would be driven through the care of Christian kings such that we would attribute suffering to that nature which is greater than suffering—something that perhaps not even demons have ever dared [to do]. 145

Although he had shown many signs, we did not at all consider [them]. For from when this evil schism took place until now, three times there appeared [the same portents from] the sun that he had shown the crucifiers at the time of the Crucifixion, as well as earthquakes, tremors, and terrifying signs from the sky. These indicated nothing other than the heretics' wickedness and what was about to come upon the earth. Therefore, when he observed that there was no reform, he summoned a barbaric kingdom against us, a people who knew no persuasion and had neither covenant nor pact, who accepted neither flattery nor supplication. This was their comfort—unnecessary blood[shed]. This was their pleasure—to rule over all. This was their desire—captivity and exile. This was their food—wrath and anger. They were not appeased by anything that was offered them.

When they had flourished and did the will of him who had summoned them, they reigned and ruled over all the world's kingdoms. They enslaved all peoples to harsh slavery and led their sons and daughters into bitter servitude. They took vengeance on them for their insult of God the word and the innocently shed blood of Christ's martyrs. Then our Lord was appeased, consoled, and willing to have mercy upon his people. But because the Sons of Hagar should also be punished [for] the action they instigated, from their kingdom's beginning he 146 made it have two leaders and split it into two halves so that we might understand what had been said by our savior. For they had unity until they conquered the whole world. But when they had recovered and recuperated from war, they then quarreled with each other. The westerners were saying, "Greatness should be ours, and the king should be from us." But the easterners contended that this should be theirs. From their dispute they were provoked into war with each other. When, after much carnage among them, they had ended their dispute, the westerners (those whom they call the Sons of 'Ammāyē) were victorious.

From [the westerners] a man named Muʻāwiya became king and took control of the kingdoms both of the Persians and of the Romans. Justice flourished in his days, and there was great peace in the regions he controlled. He allowed everyone to conduct himself as he wanted. For, as I said above, they upheld a certain commandment from him who was their guide concerning the Christian people and the monastic order. By this one's guidance they also upheld the worship of one God, in accord with the customs of ancient law. And, at their beginning, they upheld the tradition of their instructor Muḥammad such that they would bring the death penalty upon whoever seemed to have dared [transgress] his laws.

147

Every year their raiders went to far-off countries and islands and brought [back] captives from every people under heaven. But from everyone they only demanded tribute. They allowed [each] to remain in whatever faith he wished, there being not a few Christians among them—some [aligned] with the heretics and some with us. But when Muʻāwiya reigned, there was peace throughout the world whose like we had never heard or seen, nor had our fathers or our fathers' fathers. [It was] as if our Lord had said, "I will tempt them with this." As it is written: "By grace and truth, iniquity will be forgiven" [Prv 16:6].

Considering the present time advantageous, instead of evangelizing and baptizing the pagans in accord with ecclesiastical canons, the cursed heretics began a perverse conversion, converting almost all of the Roman churches to their wickedness. They revived and restored what had been overthrown. [Thus] the majority of the westerners were [now] constantly using this [heretical addition to the liturgy]: "the immortal who was crucified for us." All the churches became like barren land.

For, just as above we acclaimed our fortitude when we were worthy of it, now we should also frankly lay bare our laxity. "Cursed is whoever calls the good bad and the bad good," says 148 scripture [Is 5:20]. For that time of rest which overtook us brought all of us to this complete laxity just like Israel's: "Israel became fat and kicked. It became fat, grew strong, obtained wealth, strayed from the God who made it, and reviled the strong one who had saved it" [Dt 32:15]. The very same thing also happened to us.

The westerners seized their wickedness without a stir. And we who supposed that we held the truth faith, we were so far from Christian deeds that if someone of old were resurrected and saw us, bewilderment would seize him and he would say, "This is not the Christianity that I left in my time." Therefore, I am compelled to lay all sufficiently bare for us to know that everything that happened to us happened to us as a just judgment. We have been punished as we deserve and in accord with what we have done.

The bishops, then, forgot: preach the word; stand with zeal in and out of season; rebuke, admonish, and comfort with all patience and learning. Instead of this they were doing the contrary: commanding and causing an uproar like rulers; raising their fearful cry against those under their authority as if against irrational animals; assuming power and gaining strength not

from Christ but tyrannically from secular rulers; mixing themselves up with worldly affairs and with unlawful disputes. They
149 take care to appear [to be] priests of Christ more from conceit
than from humility. Having many running before them and
coming after them, like prefects they process on horses and
mules. This one disputes that one and that one this one with
endless confusion coming between them. They judge tyrannically and rule wickedly. They teach, not to benefit [others],
rather to show off [with] crooked words and puffed-up speeches
combined with endless chastisement. Even in letters they speak
as if with tyrants. These are the things of those standing at [our]
head.

But what should we say about those behind them, the rest of
the priests and deacons serving not Christ but their bellies, who
"do not concern themselves with the ruin of Joseph" [Am 6:6]:
deacons of Caesar and not of Christ, lovers of abominable profit
and not of faith. The sanctuaries are completed, but none open
their doors. The altars are set but dressed in cobwebs. O, the
horror! O, [God's] patience!

Then what should we say about the prefects and rulers, those
whose evil doings surpass all (for either one should speak of
them as they desire or he who speaks should be prepared for
battle): these who do not have pity on the members of Christ;
150 these whose food is human flesh, demanding not only what has
been commanded [them] but for whom even more will not suffice; these whose pasture is the poor, and like Solomon's leech
[Prv 30:15] they suck men's blood but are not sated; [these] before
whose eyes there is no thought of God; [these] who out of jeal-
ousy for one another would destroy the world. They gather,
bestow, and give to the moth [Mt 6:18–19], and, as with Sheol,
one can never sate their desire. They do not know how to live in

righteousness, nor are they convinced that they are men and rule over men. They do not discern whether they are mortals and do not consider for whom they are gathering and storing. And the greatest evil of all: they attribute iniquity to the most high, [considering him] to be a helper of their crimes. Like a calf in the grass they delight in others' toil, and they do not perceive that there is a needy person in the world. Day and night this is their contemplation: over whom they will spread their nets. These are the things of the rich.

These are the things of the judges: pride, deceit, hypocrisy, wrath, evil, and mercilessness. And what should we say about the common people? For, like sheep, everyone cares [only] for himself, [considering] neither the law nor the transgression of the law. [I] will say a saying worth remembering: "All of them together turned aside and were rejected. There were none doing good, not even one. Their throats are open tombs, and their mouths are filled with curses and bitterness" [Rom 3:12–14]. The entire decree, as it happens, applies to us. We forgot who it is who created us and who it is who saved us. We do not inquire about this, nor do we consider what he commanded us. This one was our hero: whoever knew how to oppress. This one we envied: whoever gathered wealth. For, as much as he could, everyone put on the yoke of evil. If there was someone who broke [this yoke, it was] because time or power did not obey him. For with what evils did this sinful generation not mingle? Indeed, there was no distinction between pagan and Christian, the believer was not known from the Jew, and truth was not distinguished from error. How many of the multitude of evils that we held must I relate? For all of us "broke the yoke and cut the fetters" [Jer 5:5]. I am weary of speaking. I speak and do not lie. For even if there was someone who denied this with his mouth,

151

[claiming] that what I said was not true, by all means, in his heart he would witness that my words were true.

In Egypt, the mother of magicians, magic did not thrive as much as in our time. In Babel, auguries and divinations did not thrive as much as now among Christian people. Pagans did not leave the dead unburied, as do the so-called faithful of our days. How will I recount this last thing without tears? We would consider [there to be] a way to flee from God. For who would designate these ones faithful? Who would call them knowers of Christ? Who would dare to designate them God's people? For they shout at the poor knocking at [their] doors as if at dogs. They look at the strangers wandering on account of Christ's name as if they were God's enemy. This honored monastic order, whom even demons are terrified of and holy kings hold in honor, is despised and scorned in their eyes like a menstruant's rag. This is the evil of Sodom, your proud sister, who was filled with bread and dwelled in peace yet did not help the poor and destitute. Time teaches us what followed.

You, [tell me,] are these things [so] or not? Yes, they are. But I too am among you and perhaps am even worse than you. Yet I know that these things are [so]. I also have to report other, worse abominations: persecution of priests, slandering of holy ones, mingling with unbelievers, marriage with the wicked, consorting with heretics, friendship with the crucifiers [i.e., Jews]. What, then, my brothers, are [these things so] or not? Yes, they are. We have to make the truth known.

Then return and see greater abominations than these: scorning of sanctuaries, despising the divine mysteries, contempt for holy Sunday, neglecting assemblies during our Lord's festivals, trampling the laws and canons of the fathers, abolishment of first fruits and canonical tithes. What then, my beloved, are these things [so] or not? Yes, they are. Again, I must report other, greater abominations: evil, unnecessary ablutions, fraudulent findings ascertained from magical water, rushing to soothsayers' doors, evil possession of ashes and amulets, [seeking] wicked traditions from the dwelling place of demons, Satanic influence [in the pursuit] of the illusions of dreams, strife and quarrel, murder and adultery, pillage and plunder. What then, my friends, are these things [so] or not? I know that they are. I, I am wearying of relating [them].

For this time of rest brought all these evils upon us. Although the age did not force us to this, our wickedness did. For, if we had wanted, we could have had an age of many good things: peace would have reigned everywhere, the land would have abundantly offered its fruit, there would have been health, friendship would have gladdened, trade would have doubled, children would have leaped, plenty would have abounded, wealth would have overflowed, kings would have been peaceful, leaders would have agreed, roads would have been leveled, armies would have been subdued, horns [of war] would have slept. Through whose power [would] these things [have taken place]? Through the power of Christ's might and complete mercy. And what have we done to prevent these things [from taking place] except what I previously enumerated? We produced evil instead of good and hate instead of love. We became the oppressors of our benefactors.

154

While we were mixed up with all these evils and abominations that we related above, God saw and was saddened. And in his usual compassion, little by little he began to rouse our minds toward repentance. In cities there were earthquakes; our obstinacy saw but kept silent. He showed signs in the sky; our wickedness saw but turned away. He brought various locusts devouring fields and vineyards; none among us ever asked why. The kingdom began to be disturbed; our heart was not at all moved. He devoured our strength through tribute; our thought was not a bit moved. The kingdom over us was again divided into two halves, each pillaging the other; the thickness of our heart was unpierced. He brought raiders devastating towns and emptying roads; meanwhile, like a sheep in its flock, we remained in our iniquity. Then little by little [other] things began to come to us so that perhaps our heart would be roused. He brought plague upon the oxen so that we might come to our senses; we thought, "Perhaps it is coincidence." From all about, reports of captivity and plague came to us; we said, "Behold, happenstance."

155   Thus, along with the prophet Isaiah, I too will say in the Lord's name, "Heaven and earth, rational beings and dumb animals have judged between me and my people. What else should be done to my people [that] I have not done to them? For I waited for them to do good, but they did evil. Wait a little and see what I will do to my people" [Is 5:3–4].

When the days of Mu'āwiya ended and he departed from the world, his son Yazdīn reigned after him. He did not walk in the ways of his father. Rather, he loved children's games and worthless pleasures. He devoured men's power through his vain subjugation. For Satan devoured men's discipline through profitless exertion. But God quickly took [Yazdīn]. And when he too passed from the world, one of [the Arabs], named Zubayr, was found making his voice heard from afar. Concerning himself he taught that he had come out of zeal for God's house. He rebuked the westerners as transgressors of the law. He came to their sanctuary somewhere in the south and dwelled there. They prepared for battle against him. They defeated him, and thus they also burned their sanctuary with fire and spilled much blood there. From that time the kingdom of the Arabs was no longer stable. When [Zubayr] died, they appointed his son to the emirate.

These westerners had a general, 'Abd al-Raḥmān bar Zāyāṭ, 156 and the easterners had another one, named Mukhtār. At that time the westerners held Nisibis, and an emir named bar 'Utmān ruled it. From those easterners, another emir, named bar Niṭrun, went to battle him. The westerners were saying, "Nisibis came from Roman territory and is rightfully ours." But the easterners declared, "It came from Persian territory and is ours." On account of this, there was much turmoil in Mesopotamia.

The westerners were victorious, and the easterners were driven away. The following year bar Niṭrun readied many troops and cavalry [as numerous] as sand. He was armed with great pride and was determined to battle the 'Aqulāyē. And he also took with him John who was then the metropolitan of Nisibis.

For because Mār Giwargis the patriarch of the east of Christ's church had already departed to the blessed life, Mār Ḥnānisho' the exegete had been appointed to the patriarchal throne. [Therefore] bar Zāyāṭ had promised John, "If you go with me, I will remove him and, in his place, establish you in the patriarchate." (He already considered victory to be his, for he had many 157 generals with him.) And Mukhtār, because he was angry with the 'Aqulāyē for being useless in battle, issued a command that all their slaves be freed and go into battle in their [masters'] place. When this command went out, many thousands of captive slaves were gathered to him, and he appointed them a general named Abraham and sent him to battle bar Zāyāṭ with thirteen thousand [men], all of them infantry with neither armor nor preparation nor horses nor tents. They went off with every one of them holding in his hand either a sword, a spear, or a staff. When they faced each other at a river called Ḥāzar, there was a fierce battle between them, and all the westerners' warriors were killed. Their boasting turned to deep shame, [for] they had been defeated not by men but by weaklings. And he who was prepared for the patriarchate was barely able to save his cloak. The westerners were severely crushed, and their general was also killed. Their enemies inherited all the provisions that they had assembled, as well as their wealth, property, armor, and silver. They retreated in defeat until they had crossed the Euphrates.

158   Those [former] captives, who were called *Shurṭē* (a name that represents their zeal for righteousness), entered and seized Nisibis. They ruled all of Mesopotamia, and wherever their enemies showed themselves, there would be a *Shurṭē* victory. When they had entered Nisibis, Abraham chose his brother as general over them and went down to ʿAqulā. But because they wished that one of their own be general over them (for Abraham and his brother were from the Arabs), they rose up against him, killed him and all his associates, and chose an emir from among themselves named Abuqarab.

The ʿAqulāyē regretted what they had done. For they saw that their slaves had rebelled against them. They rose up against Mukhtār and battled against him. Although [Muktār] defeated them many times, in the end he was defeated by them, and they killed him, along with many of the troops of [former] captives who were with him. But other of the [former] captives assembled and joined those who were in the city of Nisibis. Every day, [more] assembled from all sides and joined them. They conquered many fortresses, and fear of them fell upon all the Arabs. Everywhere they went, they were victorious.

From then on God began to afflict the earth. He was roused and rose up like a warrior. His sword flashed and terrified the earth. He revealed his arm, and the world was terrified. He summoned destruction upon all his enemies and began to take vengeance upon those who hated him—just as [it was described by] him who said, "I kept silent forever, will I [still] keep silent?" [Is 42:14] and "'Now I will rise up,' says the Lord. 'Now I will be raised and now be exalted. You will conceive thorns and bear stubble, in your breath ...'" [Is 33:10–11] and so on.

Because we remained in our evil and did not at all come close to repentance for all these things, [because] "the priests had not said, 'Where is the Lord their God,' [because] the bearers of the law did not know him, [because] the shepherds lied to him" [Jer 2:8], [because] every one of us turned away, [because] we said to our Lord, "Go away," he justly became furious with us. But now it was not through tyrannical kings who compelled us toward idol worship, nor through [heretical] Arians, nor through [heretical] Eunomians—rather, he himself began to battle us. Nations were disturbed and kingdoms shook from the strength of his power. "He raised his voice and the earth shook" [Ps 46:6]. For he raised "nation against nation and kingdom against kingdom" [Mt 24:7]. As [Jesus] said [he would], he brought famines, earthquakes, and plagues. He handed over a sinful generation to bitter afflictions without equal. What they had sowed, they reaped. He blew at it and it did not remain. He handed us over to the hands of plunderers. Who can count the multitude of sorrows encircling the world, especially those of plague and famine? Never before was there anything like it. For, because of fear of plunderers, people were [so] confined that they could not even move to safety.

And in the year 67 of the Arabs' rule, after all these signs and terrors that we indicated above—after these wars and conflicts by which he was [trying] to rouse and summon us to repentance (but we did not heed him)—in the year 67, that cruel plague

160

began. Nothing was like it, and I do not think there will ever again be its like.

In accord with the wickedness that has been implanted in men, they did not consider those harvested by death even worthy of graves. Rather, like pagans they abandoned [them] and fled. Then dogs and wild animals became the brothers and relatives of whoever had died and ravens and vultures their undertakers. Human corpses were cast among roads and streets like dung on the ground, and fountains and rivers became polluted. Dogs began [to eat] many of the living, and everyone saw his devastation with his own eyes. Brother did not pity his brother nor a father his son. A mother's compassion was torn from her children. She would look at them being tormented by the pangs of death, but she was not willing to approach and close their eyes.

161

This was the horror-filled sight, this the terror-filled wickedness. For, like sheep without a shepherd, those still alive scattered over the mountains in order to flee from plague. But, like a reaper, it followed them. Dogs and wild animals heaped them into bundles. Worst of all: the plunderers they could not escape. Rather, [the plunderers] wandered everywhere after them, like gleaners. They would cast them from their hiding places, tear away their possessions, and leave them naked. They did not think or deliberate and say, "None can escape from God except through repentance and turning back to him." They angrily rebuked whoever reminded them of this, saying, "Go away. We, we know that flight benefits us more than supplication" and "We repented and were not helped" and also "We cannot, even for this." For on account of the multitude of their sins men came to this utter hopelessness.

Adversities such as all of these overcame them, but they did not repent. For "the bellows have been deprived of their fire and lead," in accord with the prophet's word: "The refiner refines in vain. Call them rejected silver because the Lord has rejected them" [Jer 6:29–30]. Truly, he rejected them, and his soul loathes 162 them. But he struck us in vain, [for] we did not accept the chastisement. He brought upon us various locusts; we did not turn back. He brought upon us plunderers; we did not repent. For three months before the harvest he kept rain from us; we did not perceive this. Plagues herded us like sheep; we further increased our wickedness. Priests and bearers of the law came to an end, churches became deserted, the holy [vessels] were polluted, towns were burned, cities were destroyed, fear reigned over all the roads.

This was the first generation—that is, this was the beginnings of the birth pangs. Next [God] further chastised us for our sins, seven times over. Everything concerning us—both the words of the prophets and the disciples, and the laws' curses— was fulfilled. We were plundered. We were scattered over the entire earth. We were afflicted "like a reed quivering before the wind" [1 Kgs 14:15], shaking and quivering like Cain upon the earth. What then? Yet another blow one cannot flee or escape: famine and plague. For [when] we fled before the plague, famine overtook us. And whatever we still had, plunderers took from us. We must use the words of Jeremiah. But he lamented one people, only Jerusalem, while we [lament] the entire world. Then let us derive [knowledge] from his lamentation so that our suffering might come to an end. But we are not even worthy of it coming to an end. [See] Zion's nobles, "sleeping at the head of every street like a darkened beet and filled with the Lord's fierce anger" [Is 51:20]. And also, "the hands of merciful women 163 cooked their children. They became their food in the destruction of my people" [Lam 4:10]. And also, "If I should go to the field—behold, those killed by the sword. If I should enter rooms—behold, those exhausted by famine" [Jer 14:18]. Those killed by the sword were luckier than those exhausted by famine, wasting away like those wounded in battle.

Our weak generation was imprisoned by all this chastisement. For from the famine's fierceness men's faces became the color of sapphire or they became black and were like brands pulled from a fire. [There were] many women who renounced their children. And many women who gave birth led [their children] alive from the womb to the grave. Then there were no undertakers, for they were [too] wearied and weakened from famine. Thus the [storage] pits that famine had emptied, famine [now] filled with human corpses. Whoever was quickly overtaken by death was lucky. But lamentable suffering clung to whoever through hunger died many deaths every day. How often while opening his mouth to request bread would one die alongside his word. Many were cast down, fell in the streets, and with their falling were silenced. The wretched state of children was a dreadful sight. For the color of their faces was [so] altered that a father would not recognize his children. Like sheep they grazed on grass, hugged stones, and slept. In the morning they were found dried out like a piece of wood. Many mothers made food of their children. Sometimes, in the evening she would be sleeping with her children. In the morning, their lives were found to have been silenced.

164

How many of the adversities that have come upon us because of our sins must I relate? For due to the famine's severity, many fell and died on the road. Corpses lay in the streets; men trampled [them] and passed by. These things were from the second trial or rather the punishments for that conduct which we previously recounted. Perhaps this much is sufficient? No. "You will again be beaten and further chastised" [Is 1:5]. For the poor have perished from hunger, the orphans and widows have disappeared from lack of caretakers, monasteries and convents have been destroyed and scattered, monks roam in every corner and holy ones in every place, the iniquitous have held back their compassion, the rich look toward destruction in accord with the word of the prophet, "When will the month end and the Sabbath pass and we will open the granaries and shorten the measure?" [Am 8:5], and so on.

While awaiting all evils, the prophet says, "You will again be beaten and further chastised" [Is 1:5]. Plague again returned to pluck at them, and it grazed [on them] one by one. And whatever famine left, plague devoured. Whatever plague left, the sword struck. These torments were the punishment for our iniquity. Because in the time of our relief we did not pay attention to the fear of God, in the time of our affliction God did not remember his mercy. He had neither compassion nor pity, just as we did not have pity upon the afflictions and torments of our brethren. On the day of his fierce anger, he did not remember his holy name. Rather, he handed us over to our sins and averted his face from us. Most of all, he became our enemy. He fought us, and, in his fierce anger, he slayed and had no pity.

Our brother Sabrisho', my soul's beloved, these are the causes of this chastisement that has come upon us today. This is "our evil that has become bitter and reached our hearts" [Jer 4:18]. Having been informed by holy scripture and especially by our Lord's words, I truly know that the end of ages has reached us. For behold, everything that has been written has been fulfilled: "Men will become deceitful, lovers [only] of themselves, traitors, brutes, haters of good, enslaved more to lust than to love of God. For they have the semblance of the fear of God, but they are far from its power" [2 Tm 3:2–5]. The blessed Paul said these things about our time. Behold, they are [now] here. In accord with the word of our Lord, "behold nation against nation and behold kingdom against kingdom" [Mt 24:7] and behold famines, earthquakes, and plagues. We are missing only one thing: the coming of the Deceiver. I think that these things are his

166 birth pangs, just as our Lord said, "These things are the beginning of the birth pangs" [Mt 24:8].

Also the blessed Paul [said], "If that which now restrains should be taken away from the midst, then the iniquitous one will be revealed, he whom our Lord will consume with the breath of his mouth. He will abolish him by the revelation of his coming" [2 Thes 2:7–8]. What is "that which restrains" other than our Lord's care? Behold, today he has taken it away from men, and there is not any restoration. Rather, the ranks of kings, priests, and laity have become confused; so too those of the seasons. As it has been said, "because of iniquity's increase, behold even love has grown cold" [Mt 24:12]. For whom do you see today who loves his brother with the love of our Lord's people? Rather, all ranks of men are filled with envy, hate, accusations, and murmurs. This one speaks against that one and that one against this one. There are none who support or encourage. If [one does], it is in pretense and not in truth. For our Lord saw all these things and said beforehand, "The Son of Man will come, and will he find faith on the earth?" [Lk 18:8]. For in whom today do you see the likeness of the faithful? Look and examine from those numbered in the first rank of the faithful until me, who is the last. Begin with priests and end with laity. Look at monks and consider the minglers [in the world]. Will you find any who keeps his rank? Will you see anyone walking on his path? For all of us are walking in darkness. Therefore what other, surer demon-

167 stration do we need that our Lord's words are close to their manifestation?

For the coming of these *Shurṭē* and their victory are also from God. I think that they will be the cause of the Sons of Ishmael's destruction. Moses's prophecy will be fulfilled that says, "His hand will be upon all and the hands of all upon him" [Gn 16:12]. For the Arab's hand has ruled all peoples. And every people under heaven are among these *Shurṭē*. For, as it seems to me, by these ones the [Arabs'] kingdom will come to an end. It is clear that they too will not last. They will mingle with the kingdoms from which they had been taken captive. They will rouse them. It is likely that those who have survived sword, famine, and today's plagues are being kept for more bitter afflictions. For a distant people has been summoned against them, those whose actions the prophets also made known. For these ones will destroy them. For they strive to destroy the kingdom of the Romans and greatly desire to rule over all. It is a greedy people that has been summoned to do something unseemly and unknown.

When it is set loose from its chain, arm yourself against those things within. The senses will be a clear sign. When they have seen, they will understand. Then the earth will be like wheat in a sieve. The earth will shake and the sky darken. The entire earth will be filled with men's blood. They do not strive against a kingdom, nor do they desire gold, nor do they think of wealth. 168 For they are fulfilling God's will. And beyond them: another evil, an evil that is hidden in good like deadly poison in honey. Up to here suffices. Here is the kingdom of the Lord. For we began with him, and we have entrusted [everything] to his power because everything is from him, all is in him, and all is by his power—to whom be praise and blessings forever. Amen.

Apocalypse of
Pseudo-Methodius

Most likely Miaphysite

Most likely ca. 692 C.E.

The *Apocalypse of Pseudo-Methodius* was the most widely read early Christian text about Islam. Soon after its circulation in the Syriac world, *Pseudo-Methodius* was quickly translated into Greek and from Greek into Latin. Excerpts of its prophecies regarding the Sons of Ishmael's imminent demise were even printed in Vienna during the Turkish siege of 1683. Among late ancient and medieval Syriac sources, allusions to *Pseudo-Methodius*'s apocalyptic schema appear again and again. There is little question that of all Syriac sources, this seventh-century apocalypse had the broadest and longest-lasting effect on Christian understandings of Islam.

Falsely ascribed to the early fourth-century bishop and martyr Methodius (d. 312), *Pseudo-Methodius* is framed as his account of a vision he had when on Mount Sinjar. This vision divided the world's history into seven ages. The first half of *Pseudo-Methodius* focuses on the first six ages, a retelling of biblical and world history heavily indebted to earlier Syriac works such as the *Cave of Treasures*. The second half focuses on the seventy-year period preceding the world's end. The Sons of Ishmael are key figures in both halves.

In Methodius's vision, the Sons of Ishmael first appear in the world's fifth age, when they conquer and devastate the entire earth but are eventually defeated by the Israelite judge Gideon. The author most likely chose Gideon because the book of Judges says he freed the Israelites from the Midianites. Since Genesis speaks of Jacob's sons selling their brother Joseph to both Ishmaelites and Midianites, the author of *Pseudo-Methodius* evidently decided that these two groups were equivalent. Gideon's victory, which in the Bible was over the Midianites, in the *Apocalypse of Pseudo-Methodius* thus becomes a victory over the Sons of Ishmael. After recounting this part of his vision, Methodius interrupts the narrative to emphasize that this battle between Gideon and the Sons of Ishmael also serves as an omen for the future. In the last age, the Sons of Ishmael will enslave Christians for ten weeks of years. At the end of this period, though, they will be destroyed by the Romans (that is, the Byzantine Empire).

The second half of *Pseudo-Methodius* focuses on the Sons of Ishmael's final appearance in the world. Here the author's apocalyptic understanding depends heavily on the schema of four sequential kingdoms found in the biblical book of Daniel. By the seventh century, there was a widespread belief that the fourth and last of Daniel's kingdoms was that of the Greco-Romans, an amalgamation of the heirs of Alexander the Great, the Roman Empire, and the Byzantine Empire. By claiming that Alexander's mother was a Kushite (Ethiopian) princess, the author of

Pseudo-Methodius further expands the ethnic makeup of Daniel's final kingdom, so that it now also includes Ethiopia. But for *Pseudo-Methodius,* one aspect of Daniel's schema remains inviolate: this was the final kingdom. As a result, the author is particularly careful never to attribute kingdom status to the Sons of Ishmael. Rather, just like in the time of Gideon, their second period of world dominance will be too fleeting to justify seeing them as a true kingdom.

Methodius's vision of the world's final age begins with the Romans' defeat at Gabaʿut Rāmtā, the same place where the Syriac version of Judges locates Gideon's defeat of the Midianites. Methodius then details the afflictions Christians will undergo during their subsequent rule by the Sons of Ishmael, afflictions that will cause many to apostatize and will leave only an elect remnant of true Christians. But in the tenth week of the final age, the Sons of Ishmael will blasphemously proclaim that "the Christians have no savior." God will respond by raising up the last king of the Greeks, an idealized Byzantine emperor whose characterization in the *Apocalypse of Pseudo-Methodius* is heavily indebted to earlier Syriac texts that romanticize Alexander the Great and Jovian, the Christian successor to the fourth-century pagan emperor Julian "the Apostate." With a little help from angels, this eschatological king of the Greeks will defeat the Sons of Ishmael, ushering in a period of unparalleled peace. Alas, the subsequent prosperity will not last long, as the barbaric kingdoms that Alexander the Great had previously confined to the north will break out, issuing in great destruction. Fortunately, the king of the Greeks will soon defeat these hordes. Immediately afterward, the Antichrist will appear and deceive many. The defeat of this Son of Destruction will finally come about through the king of the Greeks' climbing Golgotha, placing his crown on Jesus's cross, and ushering in Jesus's Second Coming. Thus ends the most influential of Syriac apocalypses.

MANUSCRIPTS AND EDITIONS

Unlike many other early Syriac texts on Islam, the *Apocalypse of Pseudo-Methodius* was sufficiently popular to survive in multiple manuscripts and recensions. Additionally, a substantially revised Syriac version, now known as the *Edessene Apocalypse,* was composed within a few years of the *Apocalypse of Pseudo-Methodius.* In the late seventh or early eighth century, *Pseudo-Methodius* was also translated into Greek and then from Greek into Latin. The Greek version now survives in fifteen manuscripts and the Latin version in almost two hundred manuscripts, including one dated to 727. These had a profound influence on Western Christianity and almost a millennium of Byzantine apocalypses. *Pseudo-Methodius* was also later translated into Armenian, Church Slavonic, and eventually even Middle English.

Five extant Syriac manuscripts include the *Apocalypse of Pseudo-Methodius.* These divide into two recensions. The first appears in *Vatican Syriac 58,* a Miaphysite codex written by a scribe named John between 1584 and 1586. In 1985 there appeared two editions of *Pseudo-Methodius* based on *Vatican Syriac 58.* One was published by Harald Suermann; the other is found in an unpublished dissertation by Francisco Javier Martinez. Three East Syrian manuscripts now housed in Mardin, Turkey (*Mardin Orth. 368, Mardin Orth. 891, Mardin Orth. A*), witness a second recension. These date to 1365, the late nineteenth century, and 1956, respectively. A West Syrian manuscript dated to 1224/25 (*Beinecke Syriac 10*) also preserves this recension and shows only minor variation from the earliest of the East Syrian manuscripts.

Gerrit Reinink's 1993 critical edition of *Pseudo-Methodius* includes facsimile copies of *Mardin Orth.* 368 and *Mardin Orth.* 891, as well as a list of variants found in *Mardin Orth.* A.

Solomon of Baṣrā's *The Book of the Bee* attests to a third Syriac recension. This thirteenth-century work includes extensive quotations from *Pseudo-Methodius* that differ from those found in extant manuscripts. Solomon clearly modified his exemplar when citing it. Nevertheless, his citations provide additional information about *Pseudo-Methodius*'s textual history.

My translation is based on Reinink's 1993 critical edition. He used *Vatican Syriac* 58 as the base text. Nevertheless, because of the large number of errors found in the Vatican manuscript, he frequently amended the text using the other textual witnesses. For ease of reference, I have included in Roman numerals the chapter numbers that have become standardized among modern scholars, even though these divisions do not derive from the manuscripts themselves.

AUTHORSHIP AND DATE OF COMPOSITION

Surviving in both Miaphysite and East Syrian manuscripts, as well as those from the medieval Greek, Latin, Armenian, and Slavic churches, the *Apocalypse of Pseudo-Methodius* clearly had cross-confessional appeal. Its popularity among ancient Christians was due, in no small part, to the author's general avoidance of Christological polemics. Although this allowed the text to easily cross sectarian divides, it has made it much more difficult for modern scholars to ascertain the confessional identity of the author.

At first, many scholars maintained that a Chalcedonian Christian wrote *Pseudo-Methodius*. The argument went that the apocalypse's exaltation of an eschatological king of the Greeks who would save Syriac Christians from Arab rule must reflect a pro-Byzantine viewpoint that only a supporter of the Council of Chalcedon could have held. A more careful look at the characterization of the king of the Greeks pointed to the weakness of this argument. Although depicted as a Byzantine emperor, this eschatological figure is an amalgamation of Alexander the Great, Constantine, and Jovian. In other words, he is an idealized Christian emperor who would bring salvation and unity to all Christianity, as opposed to a specifically pro-Chalcedonian ruler.

Two additional arguments, one from geography, another from scriptural exegesis, have shifted the scholarly consensus, so that most now see *Pseudo-Methodius* as a Miaphysite work. The apocalypse's preamble states that Methodius received these revelations while on Mount Sinjar. This location's relative obscurity has led most commentators to suggest that the author's geography determined its choice. That is, the author most likely wrote from a region near Sinjar, which is about a hundred kilometers southeast of Nisibis. Originally part of the Persian Empire, this area never had a substantial Chalcedonian presence. Rather, in the seventh century it was a Miaphysite stronghold. If, as seems probable, *Pseudo-Methodius*'s author was from this area, he is much more likely to have been a Miaphysite than a Chalcedonian.

Even more determinative of confessional allegiance is a relatively obscure hermeneutical point *Pseudo-Methodius* makes regarding Psalm 68:31. Unlike the Hebrew or Greek version, the Syriac Psalm 68:31 speaks of Kush (Ethiopia) handing power over to God. Although of little interest to Chalcedonian readers, this verse was of import to a Syriac Miaphysite audience because Ethiopia also supported Miaphysitism. The author of *Pseudo-Methodius* complains that many of his fellow clergy misinterpreted this verse as referring to the entire kingdom of Ethiopia. That is, they thought that the kingdom of Ethiopia would save them from the Sons of Ishmael, a particularly unpersuasive claim given the military realities of the late seventh century. Furthermore, according to *Pseudo-Methodius*'s interpretation of Daniel's four kingdoms, the last world kingdom had to be that of the Greco-Romans, not the Ethiopians. So *Pseudo-Methodius* presents an alternative scenario. According to this text, the mother of Alexander the Great was an Ethiopian princess named Kushat. As a result, the last king of the Greeks is not simply a Byzantine emperor from the lineage of Alexander but also a king from the lineage of Ethiopia. Due to his Ethiopian genealogy, when the king of the Greeks puts his crown on Jesus's cross, he will fulfill Psalm 68:31's prophecy that Ethiopia will hand its power over to God. Thanks to *Pseudo-Methodius*'s new lineage, this psalm could now be fulfilled without requiring the nation of Ethiopia to conquer the Arabs. Because the Ethiopic church was also Miaphysite, the resulting eschatological figure of the king of the Greeks became a more ecumenical one. His links both to Byzantium and to Miaphysitism made him, from the perspective of Syriac Miaphysites, an ideal ruler to restore Christian unity. Neither the author's focus on an obscure verse found only in the Syriac version of Psalms nor *Pseudo-Methodius*'s solution to the exegetical problems it posed can be easily explained outside a Miaphysite context.

Scholars have generally found it simpler to resolve the question of when *Pseudo-Methodius* was written. The apocalypse's appearance in a Latin manuscript dated 727 and its influence on Syriac works such as the *Edessene Fragment,* the *Apocalypse of John the Little,* and the *Disputation of Bēt Ḥalē,* which are generally thought to have been written in the late seventh and early eighth

centuries, point toward an early composition date. Equally important is *Pseudo-Methodius*'s prediction that the world's end will come
ten weeks of years, that is seventy years, after the rise of the Sons
of Ishmael. If, like most of his contemporaries, the author reck-
oned this rise from the traditional dating of the hijra, in 622, this
would strongly suggest that the apocalypse was written prior to
692. A composition date just before that year would emphasize the
apocalypse's imminence. As many scholars have argued, this tim-
ing would also correspond to the consolidation of Islamic power
under the Umayyad caliph 'Abd al-Malik, his building of the
Dome of the Rock, the beginnings of his Islamization policies,
and his tax reform. These events could help explain both the
motivation for *Pseudo-Methodius*'s composition and its allusions to
increased taxation and greater danger of apostasy.

Recently, however, Stephen Shoemaker has questioned this
dating. He notes that Syriac manuscripts containing *Pseudo-
Methodius* vary in predicting a period of either seven or ten weeks
of years between the coming of the Sons of Ishmael and the end
times. He argues that the text was therefore written in the 660s,
that is less than forty-nine years after the rise of Islam. Then,
when the eschaton did not take place, one or more scribes
changed the prediction to ten weeks of years to extend the eschatological deadline. It is not yet clear whether Shoemaker's argument will shake the scholarly consensus that currently dates the
composition of *Pseudo-Methodius* to circa 692.

The *Apocalypse of Pseudo-Methodius* quickly spread and was frequently revised and updated. If, as most scholars suggest, this
was originally a Miaphysite work written around 692, its composition was likely motivated by the end of the second Arab civil
war, the consolidation of Umayyad rule, and the increasingly
public proclamation of Islam as a supersessionary religion to

Christianity. In response to these developments, the author of *Pseudo-Methodius* stubbornly proclaimed the invincibility of the Byzantine Empire and the Sons of Ishmael's imminent demise—stances that contemporary events would soon make untenable.

.   .   .

... {V} When that fourth millennium ended—that is the twenty-fifth year of 'Āhur—during the first year beginning the fifth millennium, Shamshasnakar, the king of the East, [who was] of the lineage of Yunṭun, the son of Noah, went down and devastated sixty-seven cities from the Euphrates to the 'Adruygan and all the surrounding regions.

8   He entered the three kingdoms of the Indians, devastated, captured, and burned [then] with fire. He went out to the desert of Shaba and devastated and captured the camp of the Sons of Ishmael, the son of Hagar the Egyptian, the maidservant of Sarah, Abraham's wife. They all fled from the desert of Yathrib, entered cultivated land, made war with the nations' kings, and devastated [them]. They devastated, captured, and enslaved all the nations' kingdoms. The entire Promised Land came under their control. The land was filled with them and their camps. They went about like locusts. They were naked, ate flesh in vessels [of] flesh, and drank animals' blood.

When the Sons of Ishmael had conquered and enslaved all the land, devastated the cities and villages, taken control of all the nations' islands, and floated over the ocean's waves in wooden vessels, they ascended to the regions of the west, up to great Rome, Illyrium, Gagaṭnus, Thessalonica, and the great Luzā above Rome.

9   When they had held the land for sixty years and did with it as they pleased—[that is,] after they had subdued all the nations'

kingdoms for eight and a half weeks [of years]—they became furious and raged in the arrogance of their boasting. They had [as] slaves the kings of the Hittites, the Hivites, the Amorites, the Jesubites, the Girgasites, the Canaanites, the Ammonites, and the Philistines.

At that time, there were these four tyrannical leaders, the sons of the Arab woman Muyā: ʿUrib, Zib, Zbaḥ, and Ṣalmnʿā. They attacked the Sons of Israel. When, through Moses and Aaron, God redeemed [the Sons of Israel] from the slavery of the Egyptians and they had entered the land of rest, they were yoked by a yoke of double slavery through the chastisement of the Sons of Ishmael (these ones are [also] called Midianites). When God saw the harsh afflictions [with] which [the Midianites] were afflicting them, he redeemed [the Sons of Israel] through Gideon. [Gideon] devastated them and their leaders. He drove them away and expelled them from the cultivated land to the desert of Yathrib.

Those of them who remained swore peace to the Sons of Israel. Nine tribes went out to this outer desert. But they will again devastate the land, take control of it, seize countries, crossings, and the entrances to cultivated land from Egypt to Kush, from the Euphrates to India, from the Tigris to that ocean called Sun's Fire, [to] the kingdom of Yunṭun, the son of Noah, from the north to Rome, Illyrium, Gagaṭnus, and even Thessalonica, to the great ocean of Pontus. For theirs is a double enslavement upon all the nations.

For ten weeks of years there will be no nation or kingdom under heaven that they battle whom they will not subdue. But afterward they too will be will be subdued, by the kingdom of the Romans, and enslaved by it. Because this [kingdom] will subdue all the nations' kingdoms, and it will not be subdued by

[any] one of them, because it possesses that invincible weapon that defeats everyone ...

... {X} When the kingdom of Persia has been destroyed, in its place the Sons of Ishmael, the son of Hagar—those whom Daniel calls the "arm of the South" [Dn 11:5]—[will have] attacked the Romans. For they will attack them for ten weeks of years, because the time of the end has arrived and there is no intervening interval.

24

{XI} For this is the last millennium, the seventh, during which the kingdom of the Persians will be destroyed, the Sons of Ishmael will go out from the desert of Yathrib, and they will come and all assemble there at Gabaʿut Rāmtā. There the word of our Lord will be fulfilled, which says, "They are like the wild animals and the birds of the sky" [Ez 39:17]. He will summon them and say, "Come and assemble, because today I will offer you a great sacrifice. Eat the fatlings' flesh and drink the warriors' blood" [Ez 39:17–18]. For the fatlings of the kingdom of the Greeks will be devastated in Gabaʿut, just as they had devastated the fatlings of the Hebrews and of the Persians. Thus at Gabaʿut they too will be devastated by Ishmael, "the wild ass of the desert" [Gn 16:12]. For in anger and wrath he will be sent against the entire world: against men, animals, livestock, trees, and plants. It is a merciless chastisement. These four evil princes will be sent before them against the entire earth: Destruction, the Destroyer, Annihilation, and the Annihilator.

25

For through Moses, [God] said to the Sons of Israel, "It is not because the Lord your God loves you that he brings you into the land of the gentiles to inherit it, rather on account of the iniquity of its inhabitants" [Dt 9:5]. So too [concerning] these Sons of Ishmael, it was not because God loves them that he allowed them to enter and take control of the Christians' kingdom, rather on account of the iniquity and sin done by Christians, the like of which was not done by any previous generation.

For men would clad themselves in the wanton clothes of 26 female prostitutes and would adorn themselves like virgins. Standing openly on the cities' streets, shamelessly rabid with drunkenness and lasciviousness, they would have sex with each other. Prostitutes also would openly stand on the streets. A man would enter, fornicate, and go out. And his son would come and defile himself in the very same woman. Brothers, fathers, and sons together would all defile themselves in one woman. Therefore the apostle Paul said, "Their males abandoned the natural use of females and became inflamed with lust toward each other. And they acted shamefully, male against male. Women also thus abandoned the natural use of males and made use of something unnatural" [Rom 1:26–27]. Therefore God will hand them over to the defilement of barbarians so that men will suffer the chastisement of afflictions and their wives be defiled by the Sons of Defilement.

And I looked and saw casting lots over the world these four princes of chastisement: Annihilation, the Annihilator, Destruction, and the Destroyer. The land of Persia was given to Annihilation to annihilate it, and its inhabitants to captivity, slaughter, and annihilation; Sicily to Annihilation's sword, and its inhabitants to captivity and slaughter; Syria to Destruction and the sword, and its inhabitants to captivity and slaughter; Hellas to Annihilation's sword, and its inhabitants to captivity and slaughter; the land of the Romans to Annihilation and the sword, and its inhabitants to flight, pillage, and captivity; and the ocean's islands to the sword, and their inhabitants to Destruction's captivity. Egypt, Syria, and the countries of the east will be yoked to the yoke of tribute and taxation, and the inhabitants of Egypt and those who inhabit Syria will be under affliction seven times greater than the captives' affliction. The Promised Land will be filled with men from the heaven's four winds, like locusts gathered in a whirlwind. And there will be the afflictions of famine and plague. The Annihilator will grow strong, and his horn will be raised.

Until the time of wrath, [the Sons of Ishmael] will ride upon boasting and be wrapped in arrogance. They will seize the entrances of the North, the roads of the East, and the ocean's crossings. Men, livestock, animals, and birds will be yoked to the yoke of their enslavement. The oceans' waters will become enslaved to them.

Wasteland, widowed of its farmers, will be theirs. They will declare the mountains to be theirs. Theirs will be the fish in the ocean, the trees in the forest, the plants with their fruit, and the dust of the earth, along with its rocks and produce. The merchants' commerce, the farmers' work, the wealthy's inheritance, the holy ones' gifts of gold, silver, bronze, and iron, clothing, all their glorious vessels, adornment, food, confections, and everything desirable and luxurious—[all this] will be theirs. They will become so arrogant in their rage and boasting that they will demand tribute from the dead lying in the dust. They will take the poll tax from orphans, widows, and holy men.

They will not have mercy for the poor and will not aid the afflicted. They will strike the elderly and oppress the weary of spirit. They will have neither pity on the sick nor mercy for the weak. Rather, they will laugh at the wise, mock the lawgivers, and deride the knowledgeable. A veil of silence will be spread over all men. All the earth's inhabitants will sit in a stupor and a daze. Their wisdom and instruction will be theirs alone. The small will be considered great and the despised honored. Their words will cut like daggers, and none will be able to change their arguments. Their journey's path will be from sea to sea, from the east to the west, and from the north to the desert of Yathrib. It will be called the path of affliction. Old men and old women, the rich and the poor will journey on it so hungry, thirsty, and suffering in chains that they will consider the dead to have been blessed.

It is concerning this chastisement that the apostle [Paul] said, "[That day will not come] unless this chastisement first comes, then the Son of Sin, the Son of Destruction, will be revealed" [2 Thes 2:3]. This chastisement will be sent not only upon men but also upon everything that is on the face of the entire earth: upon men, women, children, animals, livestock, and birds. All men will suffer in this chastisement—they, their wives, their sons, their daughters, and their property, the weak old men and the sick along with the strong, the poor along with the rich, the wise along with the foolish. Because God called their father Ishmael "the wild ass of the desert" [Gn 16:12], the asses of the desert, the gazelles, and all wild and domesticated animals will be afflicted by them. Men will be persecuted, animals and livestock die, the forests' trees be cut down, the most beautiful of mountain plants be ruined, prosperous cities be destroyed, and countries become deserted without anyone passing through them. The land will become defiled with blood and its produce be taken away. For these barbarian tyrants are not men. Rather, they are Sons of Devastation set on devastation. They are annihilators and will be sent for annihilation. They are destruction and will come out for the destruction of everything. They are defiled and love defilement. And when they come out of the desert, they will split open pregnant women. They will snatch babies from their mothers' laps and dash them upon the rocks like defiled animals.

They will slaughter priests and deacons in the sanctuary as well as sleep with their wives and with female captives in the sanctuary. They will make holy vestments into clothes for themselves and their children. They will spread [them] over their horses and defile [the vestments] in their beds. They will tether their livestock to the sarcophagi of martyrs and to the holy ones' graves. They are rebels, murderers, blood shedders, and annihilators. They are a testing furnace for all Christians.

{XII} For the blessed apostle [Paul] said, "Not all among Israel are Israel" [Rom 9:5]. So too not all who are called Christians are Christians. For in the days of the prophet Elijah, there remained only seven thousand among the Sons of Israel who worshiped the lord God. But all Israel was saved by them. Likewise, at the time of the chastisement by these tyrants, [only] a few of the many who are Christians will remain [Christians], just as our savior shows us in the holy gospel, saying, "When the Son of Man comes, will he find faith upon the earth?" [Lk 18:18]. Behold, in those days, even miracle workers will despair.

Many who were Sons of the Church will deny the Christians' true faith, the holy cross, and the glorious mysteries. Without compulsion, lashing, or blows, they will deny Christ and make themselves the equivalent of unbelievers. Therefore, concerning them, the apostle [Paul] also proclaimed beforehand, "In the end times, men will leave the faith and go after defiled spirits and the teaching of demons" [1 Tm 4:1]. They will be rebels, slanderers, arrogant, haters of virtue, traitors, and barbarians. All who are fraudulent and weak in faith will be tested in this chastisement and become known. Because the age itself will summon them to go after deceiving spirits, they will voluntarily separate themselves from the Christian congregation.

At that time the humble, the gentle, the pleasant, the quiet, the true, the noble, the wise, and the elect will not be sought out. Rather, instead of them, the boastful, the proud, the arrogant, the false, the slanderers, the accusers, the troublesome, the shameless, the merciless, the extortionists, the pillagers, the savage, the ignorant, the fools, those devoid of intelligence and the fear of God, those who revile their parents, those who blaspheme the holy mysteries and deny Christ, the simpletons who do not have God's wisdom in them—they will be sought out. Those men will become ministers of that age. Their false words 35 will be believed, and [people] will listen to everything that is said by them. But the true, the clergy, the wise, and the good will be despised in their eyes and be like excrement.

{XIII} For men will be under the chastisement of the Sons of Ishmael. They will enter into such afflictions that they will despair of their lives. Honor will be taken away from priests, in the church the divine service and the living sacrifice will cease, and at that time priests will become like the [common] people.

In that tenth week, during which the extent of their victory will be complete, affliction will grow strong, a double chastisement upon men, livestock, and animals. There will be a great famine, many men die, and their corpses be thrown into the street like mud, without anyone to bury [them]. On one of those days, 36 plagues of wrath will be sent upon men, two or three a day.

A man will go to sleep in the evening, rise in the morning, and find outside his door two or three oppressors, demanders of tribute and money. All accounts of commerce and taxation will come to an end and vanish from the earth. At that time, men will sell their bronze and iron [goods] and their grave clothes.

In that tenth week, when everything will come to an end, they will give their sons and daughters to pagans for money.

Why would God avert his gaze from helping the faithful and they endure these afflictions except that they might be tested and the faithful be separated from the unfaithful, the tares from the chosen wheat? For that age is a testing furnace.

37   God will remain patient while his worshipers are persecuted so that through chastisement the sons might become known. As the apostle [Paul] proclaimed to us beforehand, "And if we were without chastisement, we would be strangers and not sons" [Heb 12:8]. So too our savior commanded and said to us, "Blessed are you whenever, on my account, they revile you, persecute you, and falsely say all evil words against you. Then rejoice and be glad. For great is your reward in heaven. For likewise they persecuted the prophets before you" [Mt 5:11–12]. And [he said], "Whoever endures to the end will live" [Mt 10:22, 24:13].

After these afflictions and chastisements by the Sons of Ishmael, at the conclusion of that week, while men live in danger of chastisement and have no hope of being saved from that harsh enslavement, while they are being persecuted, afflicted, and beaten, while they are hungry, thirsty, and suffering this harsh chastisement, these barbarian tyrants will be delighting in food, drink, and rest. And they will boast of their victory. For they

38 devastated and destroyed the inhabitations of Persia, Armenia, Cilicia, Isauria, Cappadocia, Africa, Sicily, Hellas, the Roman Empire, and all the ocean's islands. They will be dressed like bridegrooms and adorned like brides. They will blaspheme, saying, "The Christians have no savior."

Then suddenly, the birth pangs of affliction, like [those of] a woman giving birth, will be awoken against them. In great anger the king of the Greeks will go out against them. He will be awoken like a man recovering from [too much] wine [Ps 78:65]. He who was considered by them as dead, he will go out against them from the Kushites' sea and cast devastation and destruction upon the desert of Yathrib and among the dwelling places of their ancestors. He will take their wives and their children captive. The sons of the king of the Greeks will descend upon them from the countries of the west and by the sword finish off the remaining remnant in the Promised Land. Fear will fall upon them from all sides. They, their wives, their children, their leaders, all their camps, and all the land of their ancestors' desert will be handed over to the king of the Greeks. They will be given to the sword, captivity, and slaughter. 39

The yoke of their enslavement will be seven times heavier than their own yoke [that they imposed was]. Through hunger and anguish they will be harshly afflicted. They, their wives, and their children will become slaves, and [in] servitude they will serve those who had served them. Their servitude will be a hundred times more bitter than their own [enslaving was].

The land that had been despoiled of its inhabitants will be at peace. The remaining remnant will return, each to his country and to his ancestors' inheritance —Cappadocia, Armenia, Cilicia, Isauria, Africa, Hellas, Sicily—and all the remaining remnant from captivity. And whoever was in the servitude of captivity will return, everyone to his country and to his father's house. 40

Men will multiply like locusts upon the land that had been devastated. Egypt will be devastated, Arabia burned with fire, and the land of Hebron devastated. But the bay of the sea will be at peace. All the anger and wrath of the king of the Greeks will be upon those who denied Christ. There will be a great peace on the earth like never before because this is the final peace of the world's end.

There will be great joy on all the earth. Men will dwell in peace, churches be renewed, cities be built, and priests be freed 41 from taxation. At that time, men will be at rest from toil, suffering, and agony because this is the peace that our Lord spoke [about] in his gospel: "There will be a great peace like never before. And men will dwell in ease. They will eat, drink, and rejoice with a joyful heart. Men will take wives, and wives be given to men. They will build buildings and plant vineyards."

During that peace, while they are eating, drinking, rejoicing, and being glad, [while] there is no evil person, no thought of evil, and no fear or trembling in their hearts, the gates of the

42 north will be opened. The armies of those nations that had been confined there will come out. The entire earth will tremble before them. Men will become frightened, flee, and hide themselves in mountains, caves, and tombs. They will die from fear and hunger, and there will be no one to bury them.

They will eat children in front of watching parents. For these nations that will come out of the north eat human flesh and drink animals' blood like water. They eat the earth's vermin—mice, snakes, scorpions, and all abominable creepy things that creep on the earth—as well as the dead bodies of unclean animals and stillborn livestock. They will slaughter babies and give [them] to their mothers and force them to eat their children's bodies. And they eat dead dogs, kittens, and all defilement. They will devastate the earth, and none will be able to stand before them.

43 But after one week of affliction, all of them will be devastated in the Valley of Joppa. For they all will be gathered there—they, their wives, and their children. God will send one of the angels' commanders there, and he will devastate them in an hour. Then the king of the Greeks will descend and dwell in Jerusalem for a week and a half. And at the end of ten and a half years, the Son of Destruction will be revealed.

{XIV} This one will be conceived and born in Chorazin, grow up in Bethsaida, and reign in Capernaum. Chorazin will boast of him because he was born there, Bethsaida because he grew up there, and Capernaum because he reigned there. Therefore, in his gospel, our Lord lamented the three of them, saying, "Woe to you, Chorazin, woe to you, Bethsaida, woe to you, Capernaum, who were raised to heaven, you will be brought down to Sheol" [Mt 11:21–23 Lk 10:13–15].

As soon as the Son of Destruction will be revealed, the king of the Greeks will ascend and stand upon Golgotha. He will bring the holy cross and place it where it was fastened when it bore Christ. The king of the Greeks will place his diadem on the top of the holy cross, stretch his two hands out to heaven, and hand the kingdom over to God the Father. The holy cross will be raised to heaven and the royal crown with it. For the holy cross upon which Christ was crucified (he was crucified for the salvation of all who believe in him) is the symbol that will appear prior to our Lord's coming so as to shame unbelievers.

[Thus] will be fulfilled the word of the blessed David, who prophesied concerning the end of the ages and said, "Kush will hand over power to God" [Ps 68:31]. For a son of Kushyat, the daughter of Pil, the king of the Kushites, is the one who "will hand power over to God." And as soon as the holy cross is raised to heaven, the king of the Greeks will hand his soul over to his creator. All rule and authority will then be abolished.

Immediately, the Son of Destruction will be revealed, he who is from the tribe of Dan, in accord with the prophecy of Jacob, who prophesied concerning him and said, "Dan will be a snake, a serpent who lies on the road leading to the kingdom of heaven [who will bite the horse on its heel and throw its rider backward]" [Gn 49:17]. "He will bite the horse" [signifies] words in the semblance of righteousness. "Throw its rider backward" [signifies] the holy ones who will turn toward his error. And "heel" signifies for us the end of the ages and the conclusion of years. With the deceptive, illusory signs that he performs, "he will bite" those holy ones who, at that time, ride on the word of truth, who are humbled and abased in the toils of righteousness. But when [the holy ones] see lepers being cleansed, [the eyes of] the blind being opened, the paralyzed walking, demons being expelled, the sun darkening as he looks at it, and the moon being changed to blood at his command, trees bearing fruit on their branches, the earth sprouting, and founts of water drying up, they will run after the Deceiver. Through these illusory signs he will deceive the holy ones. Therefore [Jacob] said, "He will bite the horse on its heel." For every blemish that by iron or by biting is made on the body, some scar will be marked on [the body for] as long as it lives. So too for every sin that is done in the soul, fire and eternal torment will be reserved for it. For "backward" indicates the left side. And when the blessed Jacob looked with the eye of the spirit and saw that affliction which would happen at that time, he said, "Lord, I awaited your salvation" [Gn 49:18]. Our Lord also said, "If Satan is able, he will deceive even the elect" [Mt 24:24].

For this Son of Destruction will enter Jerusalem, dwell in God's temple, and pretend to be like God. But he is a mortal man, embodied from semen and born of a married woman from the tribe of Dan. But if he could, through the bitterness of his inclination, this Child of Destruction would deceive all. For he will become a dwelling place for all demons, and all their actions will be accomplished by him.

At the coming of our Lord from heaven, he will be handed over to the Gehenna of fire and to the outer darkness. There he, along with all those who believed in him, will be amid weeping and the gnashing of teeth. But as for us, may our lord Jesus 48 Christ consider us worthy of his heavenly kingdom, along with all who do his will. Let us offer glory, honor, adoration, and exaltation now and always, for ever and ever. Amen.

Edessene Apocalypse

Most likely Miaphysite

Most likely early 690s C.E.

Due to missing pages, this document's original title has not been preserved. But because of its emphasis on the city of Edessa, modern scholars most often refer to it as the *Edessene Apocalypse* (or sometimes the *Edessene Fragment*). This text is a substantially abridged and revised version of the earlier *Apocalypse of Pseudo-Methodius*. Although heavily dependent on *Pseudo-Methodius*, the *Edessene Apocalypse* makes several important changes to its source's apocalyptic schema that particularly augment the emphasis on sacred space. Unlike *Pseudo-Methodius*, the *Edessene Apocalypse* specifies that both the Sons of Ishmael and a horde of unclean nations from the north will be defeated in Mecca, that the city of Edessa will remain inviolate, and that Christ's final victory will follow two reconquests of Jerusalem. It also claims that as a final portent of Christianity's coming victory over the Sons of Ishmael, a horse that had never had a human rider will enter the church of Constantinople and place its head into a bridle made from the nails of Jesus's true cross. Here the author draws from the Syriac *Judas Cyriacus Legend.* This earlier text claims that Constantine's mother, Helena, discovered the true cross in Jerusalem and made a bridle from its nails for her son. As most scholars date the *Edessene Apocalypse* to the 690s, its multiple references to Jerusalem and Jesus's cross would have been especially poignant to contemporaries, as 'Abd al-Malik was establishing Jerusalem as an Islamic center and regulating Christian displays of the cross at the time.

The *Edessene Apocalypse* points to both the continuation of Syriac apocalyptic responses to Islam and the creative modification of these traditions. Its dependence on *Pseudo-Methodius* also attests to the rapid dissemination of that text. Along with the *Book of Main Points,* the *Apocalypse of Pseudo-Methodius,* and the *Apocalypse of John the Little,* the *Edessene Apocalypse* represents a brief but significant period in Syriac reactions to Islam. These texts likely originated in a moment when the second Arab civil war and the subsequent consolidation of Umayyad rule under 'Abd al-Malik motivated many Syriac Christians to proclaim the imminent demise of Arab rule, despite ever increasing indications to the contrary.

MANUSCRIPTS AND EDITIONS

Two East Syrian manuscripts partially preserve the *Edessene Apocalypse.* The longer fragment appears in *Paris Syriac 350,* a diverse collection of biblical, theological, historical, legal, and philological tractates whose colophon dates to 1646. The *Edessene Apocalypse* is situated after a discussion of canon law and before a discussion of the technical translation of Greek theological terms. Unfortunately, at just this point the codex is missing a few leaves, and the extant text of the *Edessene Apocalypse* begins midstory. A second witness appears in *Cambridge Additional* 2054, a manuscript that now consists of only two folios. On paleographic grounds, William Wright dated these pages to the eighteenth century. Their content overlaps with about the middle two-thirds of the Paris fragment and displays only minor textual variations. Wright's 1901 catalogue of Cambridge manuscripts quotes much of the Syriac from *Cambridge Additional* 2054. In 1917, Fraçois Nau published an edition of the Paris fragment. In an unpublished 1985 PhD dissertation, Francisco Javier Martinez reprinted Nau's edition and noted all variants found in *Cambridge Additional* 2054.

AUTHORSHIP AND DATE OF COMPOSITION

Although it is now extant only in two East Syrian manuscripts, most scholars argue that the *Edessene Apocalypse* was composed by a Miaphysite author. Its emphasis on Edessa suggests that it was written in that region, an area much more heavily populated by Miaphysites than by East Syrians. The *Edessene Apocalypse* also shares the *Apocalypse of Pseudo-Methodius*'s emphasis on the Ethiopic heritage of the last king of the Greeks, another possible indicator of the author's Miaphysite leanings. So too, most scholars suggest that the *Edessene Apocalypse* was written only a few years after the *Apocalypse of Pseudo-Methodius*. In this case, its clear dependence on the slightly earlier, most likely Miaphysite text would suggest that a Miaphysite author also composed the *Edessene Apocalypse*. Although not conclusive, this line of reasoning presents a much more likely hypothesis than the suggestion that one of the few East Syrians in the region of Edessa obtained a copy of a Miaphysite text written only a few years earlier.

Because the earliest copy of the *Edessene Apocalypse* comes from a manuscript written in 1646, twentieth-century scholars assigned a wide range of dates to the text's original composition. Its dependence on the *Apocalypse of Pseudo-Methodius,* which most date to the early 690s, provides a commonly accepted time after which it must have been written. A reference in Bar Bahlul's tenth-century lexicon that seems to allude to the *Edessene Apocalypse* gives a likely time before which it was written. Most recent scholars, however, have converged around a composition date circa 692.

Several textual details support this hypothesis. Particularly telling is the reference to the appearance of the last king of the Greeks "at the end of 694 years." Unfortunately, the author does not state what calendar he is using. But if corrected for the dating of Christ's birth found in the works of other Edessene authors, such as Jacob of Edessa, this date corresponds to 692. The *Edessene Apocalypse* also includes details that many scholars see as allusions to the second Arab civil war and to 'Abd al-Malik's tax reform, additional support for a 690s date. If this is correct, the *Edessene Apocalypse* represents a revision of the *Apocalypse of Pseudo-Methodius* made soon after that text's composition.

.   .   .

... because of the oppression and evils of the Sons of Hagar. And the East will be devastated by the sword and by many battles. For nation will rise up against nation, and kingdom against kingdom, and their own sword will fall among them. Armenia will be devastated, along with many cities in Roman territory. And when of the years we spoke about there remain for the Sons of Hagar one and a half weeks—that is, ten and a half years—their oppression will increase. They will take everything gold, silver, bronze, or iron, [even] their clothes, and their entire inhabitation ... of the dead, so that the living will pass by the dead and say, "Blessed are you who at this time are not among the living." Seven women will seize a man and say to him ... , as it is written in the good news of the gospel. And because of oppression, sorrow, and famine, a man will flee from his wife and from his sons, and a wife from her husband. Rainfall will diminish, and spring water and the trees' fruit will come to an end. At that time, because of the Sons of Ishmael's impiety, all the earth's bounty will diminish.

Then, when these years that we have mentioned—one and a half weeks—have passed, at the end of 694 years, the king of the Greeks will go forth. And he will have a sign that [now] is in Rome [i.e., Constantinople]: the nails that were in our lord Christ's hands and in the thief's hands. They had been mixed with one another, and one did not know the Lord's [nails] from the other's. So they threw them all together into a fire, forged from them a bit (that is a bridle), and hung it in the church. When a horse never having been ridden, nor having ever worn a bridle, comes and of its own accord puts its head into that bridle, the Romans will know that the kingdom of the Christians has arrived. And they will take reign of the entire earth from the Sons of Hagar, etc. And afterward, as it is written, [the king] of the Greeks will hand over his kingdom to God [Ps 68:31]. Until this day, the bridle has remained [there].

Then the king of the Greeks will go out from the west. And his son [will go out] from the south. Then the Sons of Ishmael will flee and assemble in Babylon. The king of the Greeks will overtake them in Babylon. From there they will flee to the city of Mecca. There their kingdom will end. The king of the Greeks will reign over the entire earth. Bounty will return to the earth. Rainfall, the trees' fruit, ocean and river fish will [all] multiply.

There will be peace and quiet over all creation, all nations, and all people. Then the living will again pass by the dead, but they will say, "Blessed would you be [if] today [you were] among the living in this kingdom."

The kingdom of the Greeks will endure for 208 years. Afterward, sin in the world will again multiply. Once again in streets and assemblies [there will be] open and public fornication, as of beasts, and the earth will become defiled with sin.

Then the gates of Armenia will be opened, and Gog and   224
Magog will go forth. They consist of twenty-four tribes and twenty-four languages. When King Alexander saw them eating the earth's vermin, every defilement, human flesh, the dead, and every abomination, as well as performing magic and all evil deeds, [he] assembled them and forced them into those mountains and confined them there. He asked God to bring the mountains together. And it was so. But there remained between the mountains a twenty-cubit opening. He blocked that opening with stones called magnets that stick to iron, extinguish fire when they touch it, and are unaffected by magic.

At the end of ages, these gates will be opened, and they will go forth. They will defile the earth. They will take a son from his mother's lap, kill him, and give him to his mother to cook. If she does not eat him, they will kill her. They will eat mice and all abominable vermin. God's mercy will be removed from the earth's inhabitants. Men will see all sorts of evil in their days—famine, drought, frost, cold, and much oppression—such that men will bury themselves alive in the ground. If God were not to shorten these days, all flesh would die.

Some say that they will reign two years and eight months, from when they go forth until they perish. When they have gone   225
about the entire earth and reigned over the whole world, God

will have mercy upon his servants. He will gather them to the land where the Sons of Ishmael perished, that is to Mecca. Then God will command the angels to stone them with hailstones so that all of them perish and none remain. In their days, weights and measures will be abolished. Their faces will be hideous, and everyone who sees them will hate and fear them. The height of one of them will be an arm's [length].

At that time, the Son of Destruction (who will be called the Antichrist) will go forth. Through deceit and falsehood he will seize the world without [using] a sword. His sin will exceed that of Satan. This is what Jacob-Israel said to his sons: "Gather round and I will show you what will happen to you at the end of days" [Gen 49:1]. He was referring them to [this] time. What our Lord referred to will be fulfilled. That is, Satan will unite with the Antichrist. And just as the divinity united with humanity and performed signs and wonders, [so too the Antichrist] will make public (but useless) signs. He will spread strange and false rumors. Through falsehood and magic he will raise the dead and [heal] the crippled and the blind.

He will be born in Tyre, [grow up] in Sidon, and dwell in Capernaum. Therefore our Lord [said], "Woe to you, Chorazin. Woe to you, Bethsaida, and you, Capernaum. How long will you be exalted? You will be brought down to Sheol" [Mt 11:21–23; Lk 10:13–15]. Without a battle, he will reign over the entire world and say that he is Christ. Along with his following, he will go from place to place. He will have with him many thousands of demons, an innumerable multitude. He will abolish offerings and altars. Crowds of Jews will be the first to come and be led astray by him, and they will say that he is Christ. Brides will abandon their husbands and go after him. He will reign over the entire earth. But he will not enter the city of Edessa. For God has blessed and protected it. And he will not enter these four monasteries, which will endure [as] the foremost in the world. Finally, he will enter Jerusalem and the temple, as it was said in the Gospel, "When you see the abominable sign in the holy place" [Mt 24:15] ([that is], iniquity, sin, and fornication, for the abominable sign is the Antichrist). And when he enters Jerusalem, Enoch and Elijah will then go out from the land of the living. They will rise up, disputing and cursing him. When he sees them, he will dissolve like salt in water, and he and the demons who entered him will be judged before [other] men [are].

Afterward, the king of the Greeks will come to Jerusalem and ascend Golgotha, where our savior was crucified. Our Lord's cross will be in his hand. The king of the Greeks will be a descendant of Kushyat, daughter of Kushyat from the king of Kush, who are called Nubians. And when [the king of the Greeks] ascends [with] the cross in his hand, the crown that descended from heaven onto the head of the former emperor Jovian will pass over the top of the Lord's cross. [The king of the Greeks] will raise the cross and crown toward heaven. Gabriel, the chief of the angels, will descend and take the cross and crown and bring them up to heaven. Then the king, everyone upon the earth, all animals, and all livestock will die. Because his glory does not need light or anything else, nothing will remain alive, [not even] that light which God created for the children of Adam, the sinner. The stars will drop like leaves and the earth return to as it was: empty and void.

When all these creations are abolished, immediately, in the blink of an eye, the horn and trumpet will sound. The good and the evil will be gathered because there is a single resurrection for everyone. Pangs will strike the earth, as of a woman about to give birth, and Adam and all his children will go forth. No one will remain without being immediately resurrected. Then a light greater than the light of the sun will rise from the east. Our lord Jesus Christ will come like lightning and fulfill everything that the prophet David said: "A strong voice will go out from the east and be heard in heaven" [Ps 68:22]. The light [will distinguish] between the good and the evil. [The good] will see the unequalled light, the likes of which has never been seen, because there is a single resurrection for all but not a single reward. [As] for sinners, there will be no torment greater than not seeing that light.

228

Then the hour of reckoning and judgment will come. The judgment is the separation of the [good] from the evil. Language and speech will cease, and the good and the evil will both go forth for judgment. The good will ascend to heaven, and the evil will remain upon the earth. This is Gehenna for the evil. As the teacher Mār Ephrem said, "The fire is within the person himself like a hot fever. Gehenna is in them." Thus the good will ascend to heaven and to the kingdom. There will not be a single reward for them. Rather, at that time, everyone will be rewarded in accord with what they have done.

Exegesis of the Pericopes
of the Gospel

HNANISHO' I

East Syrian

Late seventh century

Ḥnanisho' I (d. 699/700) was the head, the catholicos, of the East Syrian church from circa 685 to circa 692. In the early 690s a Muslim governor deposed him, and he retired to the monastery of Mār Yunan. Most likely toward the end of his life, Ḥnanisho' wrote a gospel commentary that survives only in fragments quoted by later exegetical works. In one fragment, primarily concerned with Jesus's entry into Jerusalem, he focuses on anti-Jewish polemic. But toward the end of this fragment he also briefly refers to "some new folly" that sees Jesus simply as one of the prophets. Although only the briefest of allusions to Islam, this is one of the earliest Christian references to Islamic beliefs concerning Jesus.

MANUSCRIPTS AND EDITION

The interpretation of Matthew 21:9 by Ḥnanisho' is now found in the *Gannat Bussāmē* (Garden of Delights), a commentary on the East Syrian lectionary most likely compiled between the tenth and thirteenth centuries. A number of manuscripts preserve the *Gannat Bussāmē,* but there is no critical edition of the entire work. In 1990 Gerrit Reinink published a transliteration of the Ḥnanishoʿ passage as it appears in *British Library Or.* 9353 (dated 1892).

AUTHORSHIP AND DATE OF COMPOSITION

No one has questioned this fragment's authorship, especially as its style and content are similar to those of the dozens of other quotations that later sources attribute to Ḥnanishoʿ. It is not known when he wrote his gospel commentary. Some have suggested that because he spent most of his final decade at the monastery of Mār Yunan, that would have been a particularly likely time for him to write such a work.

. . .

If Israel had not celebrated anyone in this way—neither priest nor king nor those who dazzled with prophecy—as [it] uniquely [celebrated] Jesus, why do the Jewish quarrelers and God haters oppose Jesus being acknowledged as God? For if he were a deceiver, as their audacity [declares], how would such a person have been honored by the people as God? If he were a deceiver, why would he be acknowledged as one who came in the name of the Lord and, similarly, be blessed and proclaimed the king of Israel? If he were [only] a prophet, as some new folly babbles— [that is,] "this is Jesus [the prophet] of Nazareth of the Galilee" [Mt 21:11]—when and to which of the prophets did the people (sometimes an adult, sometimes a child not yet mature) cry out hosanna?

Life of Theoduṭē

Miaphysite

Possibly late seventh century C.E.

A soon to be published Syriac hagiography of Theoduṭē, the late seventh-century Miaphysite bishop of Amid, contains references to the poll tax and several passages in which Muslim characters play a central role. Of particular import are its narration of interactions among Theoduṭē, Muslim authorities, and other Muslims.

For example, the *Life of Theoduṭē* states that in an overflowing church, Arabs gather alongside Christians to witness Theoduṭē's ordination. At another point, Hagarenes listen to one of his homilies and constantly follow his commandments. Government officials are equally impressed. An Arab governor seeks Theoduṭē's blessing, officials from Edessa greet Theoduṭē when he enters the city, and the governor of Dara helps him build a new monastery.

A more antagonistic encounter occurs when Satan entices an unnamed Arab ruler to falsely accuse Theoduṭē of conspiring with the Byzantines. The wicked ruler subsequently apprehends Theoduṭē, drags him into a mosque, and has him beaten. That evening God blinds the ruler, who then begs Theoduṭē's forgiveness. Unfortunately for the ruler, Theoduṭē is not feeling particularly lenient. Theoduṭē curses him and tells him that God's wrath cannot be turned aside. His only concession is that, to glorify God's name, the ruler will regain his sight, but then he "will be hit again, and harder." Theoduṭē makes the sign of the cross and uses Jesus's name to heal the ruler. All are amazed, and Christians, Hagarenes, and pagans flock to seek Theoduṭē's blessing. As for the ruler, the very next day he is thrown from his horse and dies.

As these examples suggest, the *Life of Theoduṭē* is far from an objective account. Nevertheless, its depictions may reflect much more porous religious boundaries than have generally been attributed to early Christianity and Islam. Because Brigham Young University Press will soon publish an edition and translation of this text, I have not here provided my own translation.

MANUSCRIPTS AND EDITION

The Syriac *Life of Theoduṭē* survives in a partially damaged twelfth-century manuscript, *Mardin 275*. There is also a Garshuni (Arabic using Syriac characters) version that appears in an eighteenth-century manuscript, *St. Mark Jerusalem 199*. Andrew Palmer and Jack Tannous are preparing an edition and English translation of the *Life* that will be published shortly.

AUTHORSHIP AND DATE OF COMPOSITION

The end of the *Life* states that it was written by a priest named Symeon of Samosata. The text, however, claims that Symeon was not the author. Rather, Theoduṭē's illiterate disciple Joseph dictated the *Life* to Symeon. Palmer and Tannous, who have worked directly with the unpublished text, give strong credence to this authorial claim and thus date the *Life* to soon after Theoduṭē's death in 698. There remains, however, the very real possibility that this attribution is false. The text's content clearly indicates a Miaphysite author. But until at least the work's publication and examination by other scholars, its authorship and date of composition will remain open questions.

Colophon of *British Library Additional* 14,448

East Syrian

699 C.E.

British Library Additional 14,448 is one of two Umayyad-era Syriac manuscripts whose colophon includes a hijra date. This shows that within a few decades after Muḥammad's death, Syriac Christians were already familiar with the Muslim dating formula (albeit this particular scribe miscalculated the date by a year). This brief note is also important for its vocabulary. The scribe refers to his conquerors both as Arabs and as Ishmaelites and seems to use these terms interchangeably. Unlike contemporary apocalyptic writers, this scribe refers to the Ishmaelites as having both a kingdom and a dynasty (i.e., the house of Marwān) and uses Muslim political history to help situate the manuscript's composition date.

MANUSCRIPT AND EDITION

British Library Additional 14,448 is a 209-folio East Syrian codex containing a Syriac translation of most of the New Testament. According to the colophon, it took six months for the scribe to copy these four hundred or so pages. An edition of the colophon appeared in William Wright's 1870 manuscript catalog.

AUTHORSHIP AND DATE OF COMPOSITION

The last dates given in the colophon are February A.G. 1012 (699 C.E.) and A.H. 80 (700 C.E.). It is more likely that the scribe made a slight mistake with the date according to the reckoning of the Arabs than with that in the "well-known reckoning of the Greeks."

·   ·   ·

This New [Testament] was begun on the first of August and was completed when ten days had passed from February: in the year 1012 according to the well-known reckoning of the Greeks, which is [the year] 80 according to that of the Arabs during the kingdom of the house of Marwān, in the days of ... [the Ishm] aelites.

Apocalypse of John the Little

Miaphysite

Most likely early eighth century C.E.

The *Apocalypse of John the Little* claims to be a revelation given to the apostle John, the younger of the two sons of Zebedee (hence "the Little"). This apocalypse builds on the imagery of Revelation and begins with an angel presenting John with a scroll that records what men will suffer at the end of time and a heavenly voice providing him with further details regarding the eschaton. Modifying the book of Daniel's schema of four successive kingdoms, the *Apocalypse of John the Little* tells of the rise and fall of Rome, Persia, and Media. God destroys each of these kingdoms because of their sins. The majority of the apocalypse, however, concentrates on the fourth kingdom, that of the descendants of Ishmael. This kingdom of the South will conquer the entire land (an allusion to Daniel 11:5, "Then the king of the South will grow strong"). Its rule will be characterized by plunder, enslavement, and unprecedented taxation. Eventually, God will become angry with this last kingdom and will send an angel of wrath to cause dissention among its inhabitants. They will divide into two factions, and many will die in the resulting civil war. Then a king of the North will rise up against the southern kingdom. The demise of the people of the South, however, will ultimately come through the Lord, who will send them back to the land from which they came. There, without further battle, God will decimate them such that they will never again rise up.

The *Apocalypse of John the Little* presents some of the harshest surviving Syriac depictions of Islamic rule. It describes the people of the South as a hideous people, womanlike in appearance, who sin against God's creation. They are a defiled people who plunder and enslave all corners of the earth, who hate the Lord's name, and under whose reign Christians suffer great oppression, especially through the constant demands for tribute. The text also contains one of the earliest Christian allusions to Muḥammad, speaking of him as "a warrior, one whom they will call a prophet." The *Apocalypse of John the Little* may also preserve one of the earliest references to Christians converting to Islam. The phrase I translate as "act like brides and bridegrooms" others have translated as "converted like brides and bridegrooms." The verb in question (*'thpk*) can have either meaning, and in neither case is the simile particularly clear.

As others have noted, perhaps the most striking feature of this apocalypse is how strongly its eschatology differs from that of earlier Syriac apocalyptic writings about Islam. Previous Syriac writers emphasized the transitory nature of their conquerors' rule, stressing that the Arabs would not be around long enough to constitute a true kingdom. These earlier writers clung to the traditional Christian interpretation of Daniel's schema, in which the Romans (now the Byzantines) would constitute the world's final kingdom. As a result, works such as the *Apocalypse of Pseudo-Methodius* focus on the eschatological figure of the world's last Byzantine king, who would spectacularly defeat the Arabs and help usher in the end of time.

In contrast, the *Apocalypse of John the Little* reinterprets Daniel's four kingdoms as those of, respectively, the Romans, the Persians, the Medes (quite ahistorically), and the people of the South. Additionally, although it also has a king of the North, this figure is quite different from *Pseudo-Methodius*'s and the *Edessene Apocalypse*'s king of the Greeks. The northern one will neither pursue the people of the South beyond Christian territory nor ultimately defeat them. So too the *Apocalypse of John the Little* concludes not with the world's end but with God sending the people of the South back to where they had come from.

There is a more than hundred-year gap between the composition of the *Apocalypse of John the Little* and the next extant Syriac anti-Islamic apocalypse. With the successful consolidation of the Umayyad dynasty following the second Arab civil war, it was increasingly apparent to Syriac Christians that Arab rule was not going away anytime soon. Even this last Umayyad-era apocalypse seems to fizzle toward its end, replacing the imminent and spectacular role reversals envisioned by earlier Syriac writers with a much more subdued conclusion.

MANUSCRIPT AND EDITION

The *Apocalypse of John the Little* survives in a unique copy, found in *Harvard Syriac* 93. This is an incomplete codex that J. Rendel Harris dated on paleographic grounds to the mid-eighth century. The extant manuscript contains an assortment of documents, including letters by Jacob of Edessa, an excerpt from

Severus of Antioch, a lengthy collection of apostolic canons, a discussion of those who recant their heresy, and an investigation of the names of heavenly powers. Immediately after a series of questions raised by easterners and before an extract from the *Teachings of Addai,* there appears an eleven-folio work titled *The Gospel of the Twelve Apostles Together with the Revelations of Each of Them.* This collection consists of an introduction (*The Gospel of the Twelve Apostles*) followed by three apocalypses, one attributed to the apostle Peter, one to James, and one to John. The *Apocalypse of Simon Peter* is concerned primarily with polemics against the Church of the East, the *Apocalypse of James the Apostle* with polemics against Judaism, and the *Apocalypse of John the Little* with the rise of Islam. In 1900 Harris published an edition of these texts.

AUTHORSHIP AND DATE OF COMPOSITION

Although the final section of *The Gospel of the Twelve Apostles Together with the Revelations of Each of Them* is attributed to the apostle John, the *Apocalypse of John the Little* is clearly pseudonymous. It refers to many historical events that occurred long after the first century, such as the rise of Constantine, the murder of the Persian king of kings Khosrau II, the Islamic conquests, and the beginnings of the Umayyad dynasty. The last datable historical reference appears to be 'Abd al-Malik's defeat of Ibn al-Zubayr in 692. Although this establishes a clear time after which the text must have been written, it is not immediately obvious how many years passed between 692 and the composition of the *Apocalypse of John the Little.*

Harris considered the apocalypse's reference to Ishmael as the father of twelve princes an allusion to twelve caliphs. He also interpreted the text's discussion of civil war as referring to the rise of the Abbasids. He therefore dated its composition to the late 740s and suggested that the extant manuscript is an autograph, that is, the original. More recent scholarship has argued that due to Genesis stating that Ishmael would father twelve princes, the number twelve's symbolic value would have been more important to the author than its historical accuracy. Moreover, the details of the *Apocalypse of John the Little* fit better with the reign of 'Abd al-Malik (d. 705) than with the end of the Umayyad dynasty. Most modern scholars thus accept a composition date of the early eighth century.

The texts surrounding *The Apocalypse of John the Little* clearly indicate a Miaphysite author: the *Apocalypse of Simon Peter* contains a polemic against the Church of the East, and the codex also preserves a tractate by Severus against the followers of Nestorius, as well as several works by the Miaphysite Jacob of Edessa. Both Harris and Han J. W. Drijvers have suggested an Edessene origin for the work. This too is supported by *Harvard Syriac 93*'s content (e.g., the works of Jacob of Edessa and the excerpt from the *Teachings of Addai* that focuses on Edessa). Additionally, as Harris pointed out, *The Gospel of the Twelve Apostles* erroneously dates Christ's birth to 309 in the Seleucid calendar that most early Syriac Christians used, a date that commonly appears among Edessene authors.

.   .   .

The revelation of John the Little, the brother of James, those who [together] are the sons of Zebedee.

Suddenly there was a great earthquake, and John, [James's] brother and the initiate of our Lord, fell prostrate on the ground. With great trembling he worshiped God, the lord of all. Our

Lord sent him a man in white clothing, riding a horse of fire whose appearance was like a flash of fire. He approached [John], raised him up, and said to him, "John, behold, you, along with the three [other] servants of truth, have been appointed by our Lord to preach the gospel of salvation. Although none of you will be deprived of the gift [of the spirit], a double [measure] of the spirit has been given you because you made known the mystery of our savior more than your former companions [did]." John was moved and inflamed by the Holy Spirit and said, "Behold, I see the heavens opening and the holy ones in the highest heights whose appearance shines. They are praising God, the creator of all." 16

And [John said,] "I saw an angel from among those near him approach, and he brought scrolls written by the finger of truth. Inscribed on them were times and generations, men's iniquities and sins, and the evils that will come upon the earth. I stood up dazed, and there was an exceedingly terrible voice that said, 'Let the mysteries that previously were hidden [now] be revealed in soul and spirit.' The angel of the Lord who had been sent to me approached and said, 'Open your mouth and receive.' I opened my mouth, and I saw him place in it something that was like beryl and was white as snow. Its taste was very sweet, and I ate it. He said to me, 'Behold, the day of salvation and the hour of deliverance. Speak, because the Lord is pleased with you. Speak, man who has authority over God's mysteries. Speak without fear because it is God's will that hidden things be explained to you.' And I saw that on the scrolls was written what men will endure at the end of time. When I saw all that had passed, I did not want to speak about it, but [I wanted] to explain [only] what will come.

"And there was a voice that said to me, 'Woe, woe to men who remain in the coming generations and times. For kings of the

North will rise up, grow strong, and terrify the entire inhabited world. And there will be a man among them who will subdue all people with a wondrous sign that will appear to him in the heavens. He will prosper and do well. But after him kings from the Romans will rise up: despicable, evil, idol worshipers and godless, accusers, deceivers, and hypocrites. All the Romans will fall into fornication and adultery. Drinking much wine, they will love wantonness and debauchery. When their rule is upon the entire inhabited world, because of their evil sins and blasphemies against God, from heaven the Lord will send wrath upon them.

"Because [Rome] committed [so] much wickedness, Persia will prevail over it, drive [it] away, and expel this kingdom from the land. Kings will rise up among [the Persians]: great and renowned, lovers of money. And they will extract tribute from the land. There will be one of them who, on account of love of money, will destroy so many men that he will end commerce in all the land. And he will die from [the hand of] his own son. All the silver and gold that he assembled will not save him. Afterward, Persia will reign a little while and be handed over to Media. Because of [the Persians'] evil sins, the God of heaven will abolish their rule. He will blot out their kingdom, and they will perish and come to an end.

"But there will be deniers of truth, those do not know God, those defiled by wantonness, who anger God. Then suddenly the prophecy of the beautiful, pure Daniel will be fulfilled: 'God will bring forth a mighty southern wind' [Dn 11:5]. And from it will come a people hideous in appearance, whose appearance and conduct are like those of women. A warrior, one whom they will call a prophet, will rise up among them. And there will be brought into his hands ... none in the world are like or similar to them. For everyone who hears will shake his head and mock, 'Why say this?' and 'God sees but averts [his eyes].' And the South will prosper. They will trample Persia with the hooves of their armies' horses and subdue it. They will devastate Rome. None will be able to stand before them, because [this] was commanded of them by the holy one of heaven. Every kingdom, people, or country that hears a report of them will become afraid, tremble, and be terrified by the report of that people until [the South] subdues and controls the entire world.

"For twelve renowned kings will rise up from [the South], as it was written in the Law of Moses when God spoke with Abraham and said to him, 'Behold, concerning your son Ishmael I have heard you. He will bear twelve princes, along with many other [princesses]' [Gn 17:20] (that is, the people of the land of the South). [The people of the South] will take all the world's people into a great captivity. They will pillage [them], and all the corners of the world will become slaves. Many authorities will be enslaved by them and their dominion be over all. They also will inflict a great tribute upon those under their dominion. They will oppress, kill, and destroy .... They will impose tribute upon ..., the likes of which was never heard, such that a man will go forth from his house and find four tax collectors [at] his gate demanding tribute. Out of necessity, men will sell their sons and daughters. They will hate their lives, mourn, and weep. There will be no sound or saying except 'Woe, woe.' 19

"And they will become full of foul lust and will act like brides and bridegrooms. But ... will fear them. Because, in their time, whoever has will be considered as not having, and whoever builds and sells [will be considered] to be without gain. But all who take refuge in them will prosper. They will enslave those of renowned families. There will be among them hypocrites who do not know God or respect anyone except for the profligate, the fornicators, the evil, and the wrathful. Woe, woe to men of that time. They will reign over the inhabited world for one and a half great weeks, and every king who rises up from them will be stronger, more powerful, and mightier than his predecessor because their kingdom and their authority are from God. They will gather the land's gold and go down and establish for themselves treasuries in the land from which they came.

"... after a week and a half, the inhabited world will be moved against them, and God will avenge their sins [against] creation. The southern wind will become still, and God will abolish his covenant with them. They will tremble and become frightened by every report that reaches them. 'Everyone's hand will be against them,' as was said by God's servant Moses [Gn 16:12].

"At the end of their time, they will do evil against all under their authority. They will afflict, enslave, and pillage. Men will see hardship and great affliction. Three or four of them will together partake in defilement. There will be none who says or hears [anything] except for 'Woe, woe. What has happened in our generation?' They will consider the dead of old blessed and will themselves seek death. There will be none to save [them] and none to answer. They will especially afflict all who confess Christ our Lord. Because, to the end, they will hate the Lord's name. They will abolish his covenant, and truth will not be found among them. Rather, they will love evil and adore sin. They will do everything that is hateful in the Lord's eyes and will be called a defiled people.

"After these things, the Lord will become angry with them, as with Rome, Media, and Persia. Then, immediately, the end will arrive and the age suddenly [come] upon them. At last, at the end of a week and a half, God will incite destruction against them, and an angel of wrath will descend and kindle evil among them .... between and among them. One [ruler] will be raised up after another. They will form and become two factions. Each of them will seek to call himself king. There will be a battle between them, much slaughter by and among them, and among them much blood shed near the water well that is in the place previously spoken about in the book of the Sibyl.

"When the northern one hears this news, he will not boast and say, 'By my power and arm I conquered.' At that time he will call together all the people of the land and go out against [the South]. They will devastate and destroy their forces and capture their sons, daughters, and wives. A bitter and evil terror will fall among them. The Lord will return the southern wind to the place from which it came, and he will abolish its name and glory. When they enter the land from which they came, [their] enemy will not pursue them there, and they will neither fear famine nor tremble. On that day their confidence will be in the money that they defrauded, pillaged, and hid in a place named Diglat.

"They will go back and return to the land from which they came, and there God will incite upon them evil times of misery. And without a battle they will be devastated. For all the world's generations, [the South] will not [again] take up arms and rise up in battle."

... that the Father commanded from heaven concerning them .... [After] John truly said these words, visions, and revelations, the angel who spoke to him departed. And a voice said, "... your companions that they may speak with you."

Chronicle ad 705

Miaphysite

ca. 705 C.E.

The *Chronicle ad 705* is one of two surviving Syriac texts from the Umayyad era that provide a list of early caliphs, along with the lengths of their reigns. It begins in 620/21 with Muḥammad and enumerates most of the subsequent caliphs up to Walīd I. Along the way, its author commits a number of chronological errors. For example, the initial date, most likely a reference to Muḥammad's flight to Medina, is already at least a year off. So too the reign lengths of Muḥammad and 'Umar I differ from those found in Muslim sources. Like the later *Chronicle ad 724*, the *Chronicle ad 705* does not mention the caliph 'Alī. Its author instead refers to a five-and-a-half-year period when the Arabs were without a leader. The original text also skips over the short reigns of Mu'āwiya II and Marwān I. A later reader added a marginal note referring to this period as a year when the Arabs were without a leader.

Variants between the *Chronicle ad 705*'s chronology and that of early Muslim sources most likely stem from errors made by the *Chronicle*'s author. Nevertheless, the *Chronicle ad 705* provides important data for assessing what non-Muslims knew about early Islamic political history and how they interpreted these events. Of particular note is a tendency, represented by both the *Chronicle ad 705* and the *Chronicle ad 724*, to mention the first Arab civil war but not speak of ʿAlī as the fourth caliph. This suggests that, at least in the eyes of later non-Muslims, ʿAlī's caliphate was too fragile to exercise legitimate rule. A similar explanation may account for the *Chronicle ad 705*'s omission of Muʿāwiya II and Marwān I. Its author's choice of vocabulary is also instructive. He refers to his conquerors as Arabs (*ṭayyāyē*) without giving this term any explicit religious significance; unlike later authors, who used Syriac translations of Islamic nomenclature such as "commander of the faithful," this chronicler refers to the Arabs' leaders solely as kings (*malkē*), the same word Syriac authors used for other secular leaders; he also speaks of the first Arab civil war in reference to its most famous battle, calling the entire *fitna* "the war of Ṣiffīn." Such terminology provides useful data for reconstructing how contemporaneous non-Muslims understood the early Islamic polity.

In terms of its broader understanding of history, the *Chronicle ad 705* decidedly breaks from the apocalyptic works that preceded it. Earlier authors of Syriac texts such as the *Apocalypse of Pseudo-Methodius* had constantly emphasized that their conquerors would not be around long enough to constitute a true kingdom. In contrast, the *Chronicle ad 705*'s introduction explicitly speaks of "the kingdom of the Arabs." The following lines even provide this kingdom with a degree of political legitimacy, by listing its leaders with the same format and vocabulary that earlier chroniclers had used when they enumerated Roman, Byzantine, and Persian rulers. For inhabitants of the Islamic Empire, a list of Muslim rulers would certainly have served pragmatic purposes. But the *Chronicle ad 705* also points to a substantial shift in Syriac understanding of Arab rule. As the Umayyad dynasty became more stable and it was increasingly clear that their conquerors were not leaving anytime soon, Syriac Christians began to settle in for the long haul.

MANUSCRIPT AND EDITION

The *Chronicle ad 705* appears in a unique copy, found in *British Library Additional* 17,193. This ninety-nine-folio Miaphysite compilation preserves excerpts from more than 125 texts ranging from biblical books, Apocrypha, and works of the church fathers to scholia, ecclesiastical canons, and even definitions attributed to Plato. The *Chronicle ad 705* is the fortieth document in the manuscript. It appears immediately after excerpts from Proverbs and before excerpts from Isaac of Antioch. In addition to the *Chronicle ad 705*, this compendium includes two other Umayyad-era texts on Islam, the *Disputation of John and the Emir* and the *Chronicle of Disasters*. The colophon identifies the scribe as a monk named Abraham and the date of composition as 874. Jan Pieter Nicolaas Land published an edition of the text in 1862.

AUTHORSHIP AND DATE OF COMPOSITION

The *Chronicle ad 705* ends with Caliph Walīd I's accession in 705. It was thus clearly written after 705 and most likely before 715, when Walīd died and was succeeded by his brother Sulaymān. The incipit also speaks of a territorial list. As this does not appear in the extant manuscript, it is likely that the text preserved by the scribe Abraham is incomplete and originally belonged to a larger document. Although it remains possible that this short chronicle is a translation from an Arabic original, unlike the *Chronicle ad 724*, it neither preserves Arabic loanwords nor obviously depends on a lunar calendar. A Syriac origin thus remains quite possible. This is particularly likely if, as Andrew Palmer suggests, the *Chronicle ad 705*'s reference to Muḥammad's reigning for only seven years reflects a dependence on the late seventh-century *Chronicle* of Jacob of Edessa, who made the same claim.

.   .   .

Next, a tract reporting the kingdom of the Arabs, how many kings there were among them, and how much land after his predecessor each held before his death.

[In] the year 932 of Alexander [620/21 C.E.], the son of Philip the Macedonian, Muḥammad entered the land. He reigned seven years.

After him, Abū Bakr reigned: two years.

After him, 'Umar reigned: twelve years.

After him, 'Uthmān reigned: twelve years.

They were without a leader in the war of Ṣiffīn: five and a half years.

After this, Mu'āwiya reigned: twenty years.

After him, Yazīd the son of Mu'āwiya reigned: three and a half years.

[In the margin: "After Yazīd, they were without a leader: one year."]

After him, 'Abd al-Malik reigned: twenty-one years.

After him, Walīd his son began to reign in the beginning of October 1017 [705 C.E.].

Letters

JACOB OF EDESSA

Miaphysite

ca. late seventh century C.E. / before 708 C.E.

Ordained in 684 as the Miaphysite bishop of Edessa, Jacob gained a reputation for being a stickler for church regulations. Frustration at his contemporaries' disregard for ecclesiastical rules led him to resign his bishopric, retire to the monastery of Jacob at Kayshum, and, while there, write yet more legal decisions. He subsequently moved to the monastery of Tell ʿAdē. In 708 he returned to be Edessa's bishop, but he died a few months later.

Most of Jacob's decrees appear in epistles written in response to specific questions. Although not originally written as canon law, they were later collected into Miaphysite legal compilations, sometimes in the form of an entire letter, sometimes with excerpts of the questions posed to Jacob along with his answers, and sometimes simply as abridgements of his answers. References to Muslims appear throughout most of this corpus as well as in several of Jacob's nonjuridical letters.

Jacob's letters provide some of the best surviving evidence for on-the-ground interactions between seventh- and early eighth-century Christians and Muslims. Although the correspondence is not a transparent, objective lens on how things were, it nevertheless almost certainly reflects, however imperfectly, a messy world where people and objects frequently crossed confessional boundaries. The issues that Jacob addressed continued to be contentious, and his letters became a form of "living literature" that later generations frequently consulted, consolidated, and modified.

MANUSCRIPTS AND EDITIONS

A large number of early Syriac manuscripts preserve Jacob's letters. No manuscript, however, contains them all. Even those with the same letter often vary in how many rulings they preserve, how they number the rulings, and even the wording of the rulings themselves. The most important manuscripts include *Mardin* 310 (dated on paleographic grounds to the eighth century), *Harvard Syriac* 93 (dated on paleographic grounds to the eighth or ninth century), *Paris Syriac* 62 (dated on paleographic grounds to the ninth century), *Damascus* 8/11 (copied in 1204), *Cambridge* 2023 (dated on paleographic grounds to the thirteenth century), and *Birmingham Mingana* 8 (a 1911 copy of *Mardin* 310). Other manuscripts containing Jacob's letters include *British Library Additional* 12,172, *BL Add.* 14,493, *BL Add.* 14,631, *BL Add.* 17,215, *Charfeh* 234, and *Vatican Borg. Syriac* 133. Additionally, Bar Hebreaus's thirteenth-century *Nomocanon* has preserved some of Jacob's rulings that do not appear in his extant letters. Only some of Jacob's letters have been published.

Because of the disparate nature of the preservation and publication of Jacob's letters, it seems particularly important to gather all of his references to Islam in one place. I refer to these passages using the terminology and numbering advocated by Robert Hoyland. When there is substantial variance between manuscript witnesses, I present those passages that occur in multiple recensions to illustrate how Jacob's rulings concerning Islam were modified. I have also included the versions of these rulings that appear in Bar Hebreaus's *Nomocanon*.

AUTHORSHIP AND DATE OF COMPOSITION

Given the antiquity and general coherence of the manuscript tradition, no one has challenged the letters' universal attribution to Jacob. There has not yet emerged a consensus for when he wrote any given letter. For most, the composition date is difficult to narrow further than sometime between the beginning of Jacob's career as the bishop of Edessa in 684 and his death in 708.

. . .

Letter to Addai, Questions nos. 1–73

[*Harvard Syriac* 93. Near-identical versions found in *Paris Syriac* 62, *Mingana* 8, and *British Library Additional* 14,492.]

[#25] Addai: "What should be done with a holy table which Arabs have eaten meat on and left soiled with fat?"

Jacob: "A table on which pagans have eaten is no longer an altar. Rather, it should be well washed and scoured and become a useful, ordinary item for the sanctuary or the vestry. But if it is small and of little use, let it be broken and buried in the ground."

ABRIDGED VERSION   [*BL Add.* 14,493.]

Addai: "What should be done with a table which pagans have eaten on and left full of stench?"

Jacob: "A table on which pagans have eaten is no longer an altar. Rather, it should be well washed, scoured, and buried in the ground."

[*Harvard Syr.* 93, slightly amended by the near-identical versions found in *Paris Syr.* 62 and *Damascus* 8/11.]

[#56] Addai: "A heretical ruler who had the authority to punish, beat, and imprison ordered an orthodox priest to dine with him. He said to him, 'If you do not agree to dine with me, I swear by God that I will punish you.' While they were eating, the leader ordered a censer to be brought. He said to him, 'Get up and take the perfume. Beware if you don't!' [The priest] took the perfume and prayed. And because there were no faithful in that house, he anointed them with the perfumed oil. He did these things because of [his] fear of the ruler. I want to learn if, on account of this, he is guilty and if he has transgressed the canons."

Jacob: "While it is mine to say who is a transgressor of the canons, whether he is guilty is for God to know and not me. But this I will say. Priests used to transgress the canons. They also loved to take part in worldly things and possessions. Therefore they were enslaved by rulers and those holding worldly authority. So too they were commanded by them. And, out of fear, they transgressed this canon among others. Were it not for this, I would also say that he was not guilty. For these canons were established when the orthodox had both influence and authority. But now, because of our sins, we have been deprived of influence and authority. We have been handed over to those who have the authority to command us to transgress the canons."

[#57] Addai: "If an emir orders an abbot to dine with him, should he eat or not?"

Jacob: "I do not allow this. Rather, necessity allows it."

[#58] Addai: "Is it appropriate for a priest to teach the children of Hagarenes who have the authority to punish him if he does not teach [their children]?"

Jacob: "It is necessity that also permits this. As for me, I say that this in no way harms either he who teaches or the faith. [This would be permitted] even if it were not [for] those having the authority to punish. For often from such things arises much benefit."

Letter to Addai, Questions nos. 74–98

[*Harvard Syr.* 93, fols. 26b–27a, slightly amended by the near-identical versions found in *Mingana* 8 and *Cambridge* 2023.]

[#75] Addai: "Concerning a Christian woman who willingly marries a Hagarene, [I want to learn] if priests should give her the Eucharist and if one knows of a canon concerning this. [I want to learn]: if her husband were threatening to kill a priest if he should not give her the Eucharist, should [the priest] temporarily consent because [otherwise the husband] would seek his death? Or would it be a sin for him to consent? Or, because her husband is compassionate toward Christians, is it better to give her the Eucharist and she not become a Hagarene?"

Jacob: "You have abolished all your doubts concerning this question because you said, 'If the Eucharist should be given to her and she not become a Hagarene.' So that she will not become a Hagarene, even if the priest would have sinned in giving it and even if her husband were not threatening [the priest], it would have been right for him to give her the Eucharist. But [in truth] he does not sin in giving [it] to her. Then, [as for] the other thing you said: 'If one knew of a canon concerning this.' If there is neither risk of apostasy nor her threatening husband, it is right for you to act in this way. Namely, because other women should fear lest they also stumble, for [this woman's] admonition she should fall under the canons[' sentence] for as long as it appears to those in authority that she is able to bear."

fol. 27a

ALTERNATE VERSION

[Bar Hebreaus, *Nomocanon,* edition in Paul Bedjan, ed., *Nomocanon Gregorii Barhebraei* (Leipzig: O. Harrassowitz, 1898), 41–42.]

A woman who belonged to the Hagarenes says that if the Eucharist is not given to her she would become a Hagarene. It should be given her but along with a penalty that is appropriate for her to bear.

[*Harvard Syr.* 93, fols. 28b–29a, slightly amended by the near-identical versions found in *Mingana* 8 and *Cambridge* 2023.]

[#79] Addai: "During that time of famine and scarcity, because he did not have anything to eat and no one would hire him—not even [only] for his bread—a deacon joined those bearing arms, he even took up arms, and that entire year he lived with them. But as soon as that difficult time passed and there was opportunity to work, he shaved his head, took hold of his former habit, and dwelled in peace. What should be done with him? Is it right that he should minister in his former position, or does a canon prohibit this?"

fol. 29a

Jacob: "The fact that as soon as [the famine] ended he immediately fled from evil and ran to [his] former dignity showed
that he did what he did unwillingly and out of necessity. This
too witnesses to this, that although he joined evil he did not do
evil. Thus, observing his repentance, whenever his bishop wants
to, he is allowed to show him mercy and to permit him [to return
to] his former ministry."

[*Harvard Syr.* 93, fol. 29a–b, slightly amended by the near-identical
versions found in *Mingana* 8, *Cambridge* 2023, and *Damascus* 8/11.]

[#80] Addai: "When our bishop of Mardin was attacked by
those from outside [the walls], those Arabs who ruled inside
ordered everyone to go to the wall to fight. They did not exempt
anyone from going, not even priests. Then, when the battle was
raging, a priest or a deacon threw a stone from the wall and
struck and killed one of the attackers attempting to scale the
wall. I want to learn from the canons what should be done about
this. [I want to learn] if he sinned, either he or the other priests
and monks who—though unwillingly—pulled the war mango-
fol. 29b nel's rope, threw stones, and killed some attackers from outside
[the wall]. [I want to learn] if it is right for them to serve in the
priesthood or if it is right for them to be under the canon's [sen-
tence] for only a little while?"

Jacob: "That they unwillingly were led by force shows them
to be exempt from what was done. Therefore this is under their
bishop's authority. He should deal with them mercifully and
permit their ministry when it seems [appropriate] to him. But in
the matter of a priest who threw a stone from the wall and killed
while with his own eyes he looked and saw who was killed: after
a certain time during which as repentance he is prohibited from
ministry, it should be left to the priest's own conscience whether

it is right for him to serve. As for whether they also have sinned, it is not right for this to fall under 'questions' [to me]. Rather, this should be given to the righteous, impartial judgment of God, the knower and perceiver of all."

[*Harvard Syr.* 93, fol. 33b.]

[#96] Addai: "Why do we venerate images?"

Jacob: "We bow before God with lordly veneration as our Lord and creator. We venerate the cross as that upon which we see Christ. We venerate the images of martyrs and their bones as those who are God's attendants and who also plead and petition him on our behalf. And, in accord with the apostles' word, with honor we venerate secular rulers, whether they are heretics or pagans. But [these] venerations are distinct from one another."

Letter to Addai, Questions nos. 99–116

[*Corpus scriptorum christianorum orientalium* 367: 261.]

[#116] Addai: "If he is about to die, is a priest permitted to pardon someone who became a Hagarene or became a pagan?"

Jacob: "If he is about to die and a bishop is not near, [the priest] is permitted to pardon him, give him the Eucharist, and bury him if he dies. But if he lives, [the priest] should bring him to a bishop and [the bishop] impose on him a penance that he knows he is able to bear."

First Letter to John the Stylite

[*Harvard Syr.* 93, fol. 40a–b.]

[#6] John: "Is it right for a priest to give Hagarenes or pagans who are possessed by evil sprits some blessings from the holy ones or, likewise, [holy water mixed with the dust of relics, that is] *ḥnānā,* [and] to spread them on them so that they might be healed?"

Jacob: "By all means. None should at all hinder anything like this. Rather, it should be given them for whatever sickness it fol. 40b might be. For I need not say that while you should give them some of the blessings, it is God who gives them health. Clearly it is right for you to give [this] to them without hindrance."

[*Harvard Syr.* 93, fols. 42b–43b.]

[#13] John: "If a Christian should become a Hagarene or a pagan and, after a while, he should regret [this] and return from his paganism, I want to learn whether it is right for him to be baptized or if by this he has been stripped of the grace of baptism."

Jacob: "On the one hand, it is not right for a Christian who fol. 43b becomes a Hagarene or a pagan to be [re]baptized. He had been born anew by water and by spirit according to the word of our Lord. On the other hand, it is right that there be a prayer over him [said] by the head priest and that he be assigned a time of penitence for as long as is proper. After a time of penitence, he should be allowed to also share in the [divine] mysteries. We have this as confirmation: those who were baptized by water but had not received the Holy Spirit were later made worthy of [the Spirit] by prayer alone and through the laying on of hands by the head priest [Acts 8:14–18]. But concerning whether he had been stripped of the grace of baptism because he became a Hagarene, I have this to say: Concerning those things whose giver is God, it is not ours to say whether they are taken away, or indeed stripped, from whoever had received them. But this is God's alone [to decide]. He looks for their return and penitence because he does not want the death of a sinner. Rather, he wants him to be separated [from evil] and to return. So here, in this world and this present life, he will not take grace from him. But there, on that last day, [the day] of judgment, he will strip him of grace, take the talent from him as from the evil servant [Mt 25:28–30], and throw him into eternal fire."

fol. 43b

ABRIDGED VERSIONS

[Bar Hebreaus, *Nomocanon,* in Bedjan, *Nomocanon Gregorii Barhebraei,* 22, 42.]

We should not rebaptize a Christian who became a Hagarene or a pagan and then came back. But the chief priest should pray over him and a time of penitence be set over him. When he completes [it] he should share [the Eucharist].

A Christian who became a Hagarene and came back or became a pagan and came back: the chief priest should pray over him. When he completes a time of penitence he should share [the Eucharist].

Second Letter to John the Stylite

[*Corpus scriptorum christianorum orientalium* 367: 237.]

[#9] John: "Is it necessary that the church's doors be closed on the day when the Eucharist is offered?"

Jacob: "This is necessary, especially because of the Hagarenes, so that they might not enter, mingle with believers, disturb them, and ridicule the holy mysteries."

[#23] John: "If an entire village of heretics should return to the true faith, what should one do with their mysteries?"

Jacob: "They should be sent to the adherents of their faith. For this also happened to me. Once there were some Hagarenes who carried off the Eucharist from Byzantine territory. When they feared their conscience and brought it to me, I sent it to adherents of the Byzantine confession."

Third Letter to John the Stylite

[François Nau, "Lettre de Jacques d'Édesse sur la généalogie de la sainte vierge," *Revue de l'Orient Chrétien* 6 (1901): 518–20.]

From [the scriptures] we understand that Christ truly had come. And we say that if he truly had come, from the line of David he became manifest in the flesh, just as the prophets said concerning him. If he had come and from the line of David became manifest, by all means he also came in his time. If he had come and came in his time, and from the line of David became manifest in the flesh, then also, by all means, his birth is from the line of David. Thus these things all depend on one another, are bound like [links in a] chain, are affirmed and result from compelling arguments, and there is no doubt concerning them.

That Christ is from the line of David is acknowledged by all: that is, by the Jews as well as by the Hagarenes, as well as by all Christians who confess that from human nature he was enfleshed and became incarnate. Thus this, then, that in the flesh Christ is from the line of David (as was previously written by the holy prophets) is acknowledged and foundational to all of them: that is, to the Jews, as well as to the Hagarenes, as well as to the Christians.

I have said that this is foundational to and is confessed by the Jews, even though they deny the true Christ who truly came. But concerning him whom they await to be revealed, by all means they say and affirm that he is and will be from the line of David. So too the Hagarenes. They do not know or want to say that the true Christ who came and who is acknowledged by Christians is God and the son of God. Nevertheless, they all firmly confess that he truly is the Christ who was to come and who was foretold by the prophets. Concerning this they have no dispute with us, rather with the Jews. Both in thought and in word they are united and reprovingly and contentiously stand firm against [the Jews]. For, as I previously wrote, they already knew what had been acknowledged by the prophets: Christ would be born from David, as well as Christ who came was also born from Mary. Indeed, it is truly acknowledged by the Hagarenes, and none of them dispute this. Always saying to everyone that Jesus, the son of Mary, truly is the Christ, they also call him the Word of God, in accord with the holy scriptures. But because they are not able to distinguish word from spirit, in their ignorance they add that he is the spirit of God, *519* just as [because of their ignorance] they do not consent to call Christ God or the son of God.

Then, if all these things are acknowledged without controversy, that is both by us and by the Hagarenes—namely that Christ was born from the line of David, as the prophets said, that Christ was born from Mary, that this one who was born from her is truly the Christ, as opposed to the one whom the Jews await—then it should also be confirmed both by us and by the Hagarenes that he came in his time. Then after these things have been acknowledged by the two parties, what is it that opposes, calls into question, or is at all difficult concerning whether we should say that Mary is from the line of David? For this is clear and without dispute....

... Then I declare that, even if this is not demonstrated by the scriptures, by a compelling and true syllogism like this we should demonstrate to every Christian or Hagarene who inquires that the holy Virgin Mary, the bearer of God, is from the line of David ....

.... Brother, lover of God and lover of truth, I want the truth to be witnessed by this compelling and true syllogism established by us and not by words from superfluous stories. If there should be some man—whether he should be a Hagarene or a Christian—who converses with you, asks you, and inquires about this, if he is rational and at all possesses a rational mind, he will understand the syllogism. When he hears it, without dispute and of his own accord he will witness the truth. These things that have been said suffice to clearly show a Christian or a Hagarene who disputes this [subject] that the holy Virgin Mary was from the line of David.

520

Fourth Letter to John the Stylite

[*BL Add.* 12,172, fol. 124a.]

"Why do the Jews worship toward the south?" Behold, I say to you that this question is in vain and what was asked is not true. For Jews do not worship toward the south, just as Hagarenes also do not. For as I saw them with my own eyes and as I am now writing to you, behold, those Jews who live in Egypt as well as those Hagarenes who are there were worshiping toward the east. Even now the two people worship [likewise], the Jews toward Jerusalem but the Hagarenes toward the Ka'ba. Those Jews who are south of Jerusalem worship toward the north, and also the Hagarenes there worship toward the east, toward the Ka'ba.

Those south of the Ka'ba worship toward the north, toward [that] place. Indeed, from all these things that have been said it becomes apparent that here, in the regions of Syria, the Jews and the Hagarenes do not worship toward the south, rather toward Jerusalem and the Ka'ba, their races' ancestral place.

Canon 30

[*Harvard Syr.* 93, fol. 24a–b, slightly amended by the near-identical version in *Mingana* 8.]

In accord with the holy apostle [Paul]'s commandment, before clergy and without any strife or blows, [clergy or monks] should judge and examine their actions intelligently, soberly, justly, in the fear of God, as it is proper for Christ's brothers. For when one had a suit with his brother and dared to bring the suit before outsiders and not before the clergy, [Paul] spoke censoring and reprimanding those who behaved foolishly like this. Although he said these things to Christian laity, if he had commanded this for laity, how much more should clergy and monks not bring worldly suits against their adversaries. If they are monks who have a suit, loving one another, their suit should be altogether unnecessary. So, if having some suit like this a clergy or monk dares to bring it out before secular judges for judgment and hands his brother over to blows and lashes, he should be judged as an enemy of Christ's laws and should receive a censure from the ecclesiastical canons appropriate for his folly.

fol. 24b

ABRIDGED VERSION

[*Corpus scriptorum christianorum orientalium* 367: 272.]

When clerics have suits, they should bring them not to outsiders, rather to the judgments of the holy church.

Excerpted Canon in Bar Hebreaus's Nomocanon

[Bar Hebreaus, *Nomocanon*, Bedjan, *Nomocanon Gregorii Barhebraei*, 21–22.]

Costly goods that depict pagan tales of gods and goddesses will not be used as a covering for a holy table. If they are used, they will be torn apart. So too [they will not be used] either for clerical vestments or hangings, nor [will] those that have a Hagarene confession of faith written on them.

Chronicle

JACOB OF EDESSA

Miaphysite

ca. 692 C.E. / before 708 C.E.

In the 690s, Jacob the Miaphysite bishop of Edessa completed his *Chronicle,* a continuation of the famous fourth-century *Chronicle* by Eusebius. After an introduction that corrects some of Eusebius's work, Jacob followed Eusebius's format and arranged the remainder of his *Chronicle* around a central chronological table. This table provides the regnal years of the Byzantine, Sasanian, and—in the last entries—Muslim rulers. Jacob further divided his chart into four-year Olympiads. He also added his own sequence of years, whose first year begins circa 327 C.E. According to this idiosyncratic system of dating, Muḥammad first appears around the year 293 of Jacob's sequence. Around this central table Jacob included two columns of brief entries. One is mainly for ecclesiastical notices, the other for world history, although Jacob did not always adhere to this schema.

The only extant manuscript that preserves Jacob's *Chronicle* is very fragmentary. The last surviving entry in the chronological table equates the twenty-first year of Heraclius (630), the second year of Ardashir III (629), and the third year of Abū Bakr (634). As this assortment of dates suggests, the correspondence between the various chronological systems that Jacob used was not always precise, and Jacob's account has a number of chronological errors. So too, its brief descriptions of Muḥammad and Abū Bakr seem to be at least a bit off. Jacob assigned Muḥammad's reign a length of seven years, as opposed to the more commonly attested ten. If his reference to Arab raids is an allusion to the beginning of the conquests, these also were dated early. Despite the chronological discrepancies, Jacob's brief entries concerning Islam remain particularly important for their terminology and their discussion of Muḥammad. The *Chronicle* also suggests that Jacob had at least indirect access to no longer extant early Islamic historiography, a line of transmission more fully attested by slightly later Syriac caliph lists, such as the *Chronicle ad 724*.

MANUSCRIPT AND EDITION

Sections of Jacob's *Chronicle* survive in only a single manuscript, *British Library Additional* 14,685. On paleographic grounds, William Wright dated this manuscript to the tenth or eleventh century. Unfortunately, the manuscript is missing numerous pages, and the extant twenty-three folios preserve only the beginning of the *Chronicle* and a section from its latter part. Even these are only partially preserved, due to damage to the manuscript. Later Syriac authors occasionally quoted Jacob's *Chronicle*, allowing one to reconstruct parts of the missing sections. Ernest Walter Brooks published an edition of the text in 1904.

AUTHORSHIP AND DATE OF COMPOSITION

The manuscript's title identifies its author as "Jacob the lover of toil," an epithet that Jacob of Edessa frequently used. Medieval writers confirm his authorship of this work, not only stating that Jacob of Edessa wrote a chronicle but also quoting sections from it that are similar to those found in the British Library manuscript. According to Michael the Syrian (d. 1199), his copy of the *Chronicle* contained not only Jacob's original writings but also a continuation by another scholar that noted events up to 710 (two years after Jacob's death). As for when Jacob completed the work, Michael quotes a passage from the ninth-century Theodosius of Edessa which states that it was under the reign of Justinian II (r. 685–95). The East Syrian writer Elias of Nisibis (d. 1049) narrows this time period by stating that Jacob composed his work in 691/92, although there is some contention as to whether he was referring to Jacob's *Chronicle* or to a no longer extant *Chronicon* (that is, calendar).

•   •   •

	Total	Of the Romans	Of the Persians
	293	8	28
	294	9	29
	295	10	30
	296	11	31

Isaiah is sent from the Persian empire to Edessa [as] bishop. In Alexandria, the faithful made Andronicus their bishop.

Muḥammad goes down on business to the land of Palestine and [the lands] of the Arabians, the Phoenicians, and the Tyrians. There was a heavenly eclipse. The Persians took captives and destroyed the entire land of the Romans as far as Bithynia, Asia, and the sea of Pontus.

In Alexandria, Benjamin ruled as bishop to the faithful.

Muḥammad, the first king of the Arabians, ruled ~~~~~~~ 7 years ~~~~~~~

Khosrau [II] issued a command and Edessa went down into exile.

304

| 940 of the Greeks |

While Heraclius, the king of the Romans, entered [his] eleventh year and, Khosrau, the king of the Persians, [entered his] thirty-first, the kingdom of the Arabians, those whom we call the Arabs, began.

	Olympiad	350	[621–25]
297	12	32	1
298	13	33	2
299	14	34	3
300	15	35	4

Cyrus carried out a persecution against the faithful in Alexandria. The faithful in the East made John patriarch.

— — — —

The Arabs began to make raids into the land of Palestine.

	Olympiad	351	[625–29]
301	16	36	5
302	17	37	6
303	18	38	7

The years of Shahrbarāz, Boran, Khosrau [III], Peroz, Azarmig, and Hormizdas are approximately two.

#21 [of the Persians]. Siroes Son of Khosrau, nine months

The Persians killed Khosrau and made Shiroe king [for] nine months.

#2 of the Arabs, Abū Bakr, two years, seven months				Those Edessenes who were [still] alive returned from exile.
304	19	1	1	Hera[clius] made [a covenant] with Shahrbarāz and it was decided that the Per[sians would leave] the land [of the Romans] and go [down to their land].
#22 of the Persians, Ardashir, son of Siroes, one year, ten months				
Olympiad 352 [629–33]				the Je[ws] …

Scholia

JACOB OF EDESSA

Miaphysite

ca. late seventh century C.E. / before 708 C.E.

Jacob the Miaphysite bishop of Edessa (d. 708) became renowned as an interpreter of scripture and even produced biblical translations. His extant exegetical writings include passages found in his letters, his *Commentary on the Octateuch,* his *On the Hexameron,* and his revised Syriac translations of Genesis and Samuel. They are also preserved in a collection of excerpts known as Jacob's *Scholia,* a compilation that contains a few dozen of his interpretations of particular biblical passages. In one of these scholia, an interpretation of 1 Kings 14:21–28, he directly refers to Arab rule. Although brief, this passage provides an important example of how seventh-century Syriac Christians interpreted the Islamic conquests through the lens of biblical history.

MANUSCRIPT AND EDITION

Jacob's scholion on 1 Kings 14 appears in a collection preserved in *British Library Additional* 14,483. On paleographic grounds, William Wright dated this manuscript to the ninth century. George Phillips published an edition of Jacob's *Scholia* in 1864.

AUTHORSHIP AND DATE OF COMPOSITION

Because the scholia are explicitly attributed to Jacob and their exegesis and style resemble those of his other writings, all modern scholars have accepted them as authentic. It remains unclear, however, how long before his death in 708 Jacob wrote these. In the last decade of his life, he worked on several projects that revised earlier biblical translations. As part of this revision process, earlier Greek translations of the Hebrew Bible increasingly influenced his translations. Some modern scholars therefore suggest that the biblical quotations in the *Scholia* represent an earlier stage in this process, as they neither reflect as strong a Greek influence as do many of Jacob's last writings nor follow the biblical translations that he made during the last years of his life. As a result, the *Scholia* is more likely to have been written in the 690s than in the early 700s.

·   ·   ·

The fourteenth scholion concerning the following: "Rehoboam, the son of Solomon, reigned over Judah. Rehoboam was forty-six years old when he [began to] reign. For seventeen years he reigned over Jerusalem, that city in which the Lord had chosen from among all the tribes of Israel to establish his name. The name of his Ammonite mother was Maacah. Rehoboam and

Judah did what is evil before the Lord" [1 Kings 14:21–22], and so on.

From these words it is shown that even if Jeroboam had not made those calves of gold that he made and by them caused Israel to sin, all the Sons of Israel were [still] prepared to stray from the Lord and to go after the error and abomination of the nations, those who revere demons. For behold, the Sons of Judah, who were not subject to Jeroboam: because their desire also was to stray from the Lord and serve the gods of the nations, they did greater evil than Jeroboam and the Sons of Israel. For, as well as despising God and worshiping idols, they also despised and defiled Jerusalem, the city that God had chosen and that his name had proclaimed. Therefore, because it wants to show all of [Rehoboam's] evil and iniquity, when his scriptural story said that Rehoboam reigned, it also called him the son of Solomon, he who had abandoned the Lord and served idols. It also makes known that [Rehoboam] reigned over that city which the Lord had chosen from among all the tribes of Israel to there establish his name. As one would say, both he and, along with him, the Sons of Judah, over whom he reigned, despised and defiled even this holy place. He also was the son of the Ammonite woman who had made his father Solomon erect an idol and high place to Milcom, the abomination of the Sons of Ammon. [She had made Solomon] worship and make sacrifices to him. [The scriptural story says] this to indicate the paganism and error that was learned from his father and his mother. [Rehoboam] did and accomplished more [evil] than had his father and also more than had his seducing and iniquitous brother Jeroboam, who had made Israel sin. Thus both Rehoboam and the Sons of Judah, who were designated as the Lord's portion and the House of David and [who] were in the Lord's holy city Jerusalem—although they were designated as

26

his—they sinned, acted wickedly, and did what is evil before the Lord.

They also represented a type and a figure. By their designation and small number [they represent] this small and confessing people who have been called, who are orthodox, and who confess the Lord Christ. And although they are in the church, God's city Jerusalem, which the Lord chose and sanctified more than all the nations of the earth, through their deeds and very iniquitous conduct they angered him more than all the nations [had]. For having been designated and being his, they scandalize everyone as well as the faith such that [God] also says, "Because of you, my name is blasphemed among the nations," as well as "You have despised and defiled the church, the city of Jerusalem that I had chosen," and "You made my house a den of thieves" [Mt 2:13; Mk 11:17; Lk 19:46]. Thus we who are designated the true Christians and confessors of the Lord, [who are] in the Lord's house, [who are] Jacob his portion, Israel his inheritance, a people seeing God, a holy nation, a royal priesthood—it is we who sin more than everyone and [we] who are deprived of all virtue, good conduct, love, peace, and unity. These [are the things] that, when they appeared in us, they showed us to be Christ's disciples. In their absence, they make known that we are Christ's adversaries, trampling his laws and those commandments that he taught us.

Therefore, because of the evil of Rehoboam and of Judah, God brought upon them Shishak, the reigning king of Egypt. As divine scripture tells, because of their sins and provocation, he took them captive, scattered them, and destroyed their cities. So also we, because of our sins and many iniquities, Christ handed us over and enslaved us under the harsh yoke of the Arabians— those who do not confess Christ-God and God's son to be God and God's son, he who redeemed us with his blood from the bondage of sin. Through his cross, he saved us from the slavery of the Adversary and demons. Through his death, he freed us and delivered us from corruption and death and gave us the sure hope of resurrection from the dead. He promised us the blessed life of the world to come and a portion and an inheritance in the kingdom of heaven. Because we did not consider all this grace and freedom that had been given us but became unjust and deniers of grace, just like ancient Judah, we were handed over to bondage and servitude, to pillage and captivity.

Against the Armenians

JACOB OF EDESSA

Miaphysite

ca. late seventh century C.E. / before 708 C.E.

A medieval Christian compiled excerpts from earlier patristic authors in the form of an imaginary dialogue between a student and a variety of theological luminaries such as Evagrius Ponticus, John Chrysostom, Basil of Caesarea, and Severus of Antioch. In the midst of this dialogue appears three folios' worth of material attributed to Jacob the Miaphysite bishop of Edessa (d. 708). The majority of this excerpt consists of his diatribe against Armenian Christians. As part of this invective, Jacob portrays Armenian rituals as an amalgamation of practices found in groups that he considered particularly undesirable, such as Jews, Chalcedonians, and East Syrians. The last of his comparisons is between the Armenians and the Arabs. Jacob here refers to the Arabs as circumcised and as making three genuflections to the south. Though brief, this passage provides one of the earliest witnesses to Muslim ritual practice.

MANUSCRIPTS AND EDITIONS

This short text appears in *Florence Syriac* 62 (dated 1360) and *Paris Syriac* III (dated on paleographic grounds to the six-teenth century). Stefano Assemani published an edition based on the Florence manuscript in 1742. The more commonly cited edition is that of the Paris manuscript made by Carl Kayser in 1886.

AUTHORSHIP AND DATE OF COMPOSITION

Both manuscripts attribute this excerpt to Jacob of Edessa, and no reason has emerged to challenge this attribution. It is not known, however, when he wrote the text.

.   .   .

4   From the world's beginning, the Armenian people have lived lawlessly. From them came neither teachers nor monks nor any-one who had sufficient knowledge. And because foreign teachers swayed them, they separated from the true faith. Some of their teachers were Jews and some of them Phantasiasts. Therefore they agree with the Jews in offering a lamb, unleavened bread, and unmixed wine and in blessing salt. They [also] agree with the Jews in things worse than these. They agree with the Chal-cedonians in crossing with two [fingers]. They agree with the Nestorians in crossing from right to left with the entire hand. They agree with the Arabs in making three genuflections toward the south when they offer [the Eucharist], and they cir-cumcise. When someone dies, by all means they agree with the pagans in making a sacrifice on his behalf. By this they

particularly anger God because it is entirely impermissible for a Christian to offer a sacrifice on behalf of the dead on the day of his death. For this is a pagan, truly a Jewish, custom and is foreign to the church of God.

Kāmed Inscriptions

East Syrian

714/15 C.E.

A 1934 archeological survey in modern-day Lebanon discovered thirty-one early eighth-century Syriac inscriptions at the ancient site of Kāmed. Although short and often fragmentary, these inscriptions bear witness to a group of mainly East Syrian stoneworkers whom the caliph Walīd hired to reopen the quarry at Kāmed. Their inscriptions include references to priests and deacons who came along with them, as well as "the head of the table." This phrase appears in no other known Syriac text. Some scholars have suggested that it refers to the director of a group of monks, implying a monastic origin for these stoneworkers. Others have seen the title as belonging to the foreman or to the person who presided at a common meal, suggesting that these inscriptions were made simply by a community of workmen.

Four inscriptions directly refer to Hagarenes, Saracens, Arabs, or specific Muslim rulers and provide some of our earliest examples of Christian use of the Muslim calendar. More important, taken as a whole, these inscriptions provide a rare peek into the types of substantial population shifts (in this case East Syrians to Lebanon) that early Islamic rule and Umayyad building projects brought about.

EDITION

Paul Mouterde published an edition of the inscriptions in 1939.

AUTHORSHIP AND DATE OF COMPOSITION

Most of the place-names that the inscriptions mention are in northern Iraq and in areas that East Syrians dominated. So too, several of the names of ecclesiastical officials were particularly common among East Syrians. There is, however, also a Greek inscription that refers to an *actionarios* from Edessa named George, who is more likely to have been a Miaphysite. This led the excavators to suggest a mixed group of workers, consisting primarily of East Syrians from the Kurdistan region but also including, and perhaps led by, Miaphysites from closer by. Five of the inscriptions cite the year 86. Four of these refer to it as either a "year of the Hagarenes" or a "year of the Arabs' rule." The other has a lacuna but most likely originally included the phrase "of the Arab's rule." The eighty-sixth year after the hijra corresponds with 714/15 C.E. The inscriptions also mention Walīd, who was the caliph until 715. As there are no later inscriptions by this group at this site, the excavators hypothesized that the quarry was shut down soon after Walīd's death.

·   ·   ·

[#10] In the eighty-sixth year of the Hagarenes, during the reign of Walīd, son of 'Abd al-Malik, emir of the Saracens, this quarry was opened by Gezirat Kurdu ...

[#20] In the eighty-sixth year of the Arabs' rule, "the head of the table" leveled the rock ...

[#21] In the eighty-sixth year of the Arabs' rule ...

[#28] In the eighty-sixth year of the Hagarenes, in the days of Walīd, emir of the Hagarenes, they began work ...

Chronicle of Disasters

Miaphysite

ca. 716 C.E.

This far from uplifting chronicle begins with the heading "The various afflictions that came upon the land in the year 1024 according to the reckoning of Alexander [712 C.E.] and those [afflictions that came] afterward." Modern scholars most often refer to it by the shorter, ominous, albeit apt title *Chronicle of Disasters.*

The *Chronicle's* inventory of calamities begins with a comet's appearance "when the kingdom of the Sons of Ishmael held power and its control stretched over the entire land, in the days of Walīd, son of Malik, son of Marwān, who reigned at that time." One has to make it through a plague, a drought, a locust infestation, a hurricane, a hailstorm, and several earthquakes before encountering the second reference to Arab rule, when Walīd dies and is succeeded by his brother Sulaymān. The list ends fairly anticlimactically, with a hailstorm killing a number of birds. Far more interesting than the fowls' unfortunate fate is the way the author interweaves these natural catastrophes with the two references to Umayyad caliphs. The text does not explicitly link the kingdom of the Sons of Ishmael with the other listed items. Nevertheless, the intercalation of these two rulers in the midst of more conventional misfortunes certainly suggests that these caliphs were part of God's chastisement for Christian sin.

MANUSCRIPT AND EDITION

The *Chronicle of Disasters* appears in a unique Miaphysite codex, *British Library Additional* 17,193. According to the colophon, the scribe Abraham wrote the manuscript in 874. Most scholars have categorized Abraham's collection of 125 documents as a miscellany. Nevertheless, there appears to have been some method to his madness, especially when he put the *Chronicle of Disasters* directly after another document about Islam, the *Disputation of John and the Emir*. Given that only three of the 125 texts that Abraham collected explicitly speak of Islam, the chance of any two of them randomly following each other is quite small. More likely by far is that he deliberately positioned these documents next to each other. By placing *The Chronicle of Disasters* directly after *John and the Emir's* multipage discussion of Muslim theological challenges to Christianity, this ninth-century scribe created the impression that catastrophes naturally follow in Islam's wake. François Nau published an edition of the text in 1915.

AUTHORSHIP AND DATE OF COMPOSITION

The inclusion of this document in a Miaphysite manuscript along with its referring to the Miaphysite patriarch Elijah as "orthodox" clearly indicates its confessional affiliation. The chronicle ends with an entry for Monday, April 20, 716, and was probably written soon after that date. That April 20, 716, was indeed a Monday provides additional support for this hypothesis.

· · ·

Next, the various afflictions that came upon the land in the year 1024 according to the reckoning of Alexander [712 C.E.] and those [afflictions that came] afterward.

When the kingdom of the Sons of Ishmael held power and its control stretched over the entire land, in the days of Walīd, son of Malik, son of Marwān, who reigned at that time, 254 and [when] the patriarch of the apostolic faith of the orthodox Elijah (who was from the monastery of Gubbā Barrayā, [also] called "in the wilderness") was known throughout the entire land of Syria—in the year 1023 according to the reckoning of the Greeks [712 C.E.], on August 8—a sign appeared in the sky. [It was] in the shape of some sort of long lance [with] a broad upper head. It appeared in the evening, around the second hour, in the northern side [of the sky], facing and bent toward the southern [side].

The following year, in the year 1024 [713 C.E.], in the months of December, [January,] and February, the land was sentenced to great pestilence, and many people perished without mercy. Before this aforementioned sentence had come to an end, in the month of February of that year, early in the morning of Tuesday the 28th, there was a tremor and a great earthquake, causing the houses in the towns, the churches, and many great cities to collapse on their inhabitants, killing them in many various and terrible [ways]. Some of the houses in the towns and the cities caved in. Some of the people were smothered, some were crushed, many [initially] remained [alive,] their houses [soon] becoming their graves, [and] some escaped. All these things happened in accord with the just, incomprehensible, and astonishing judgments of God.

But, [as we know] through the report and story that came to us from those men who were present and even saw [it], even this happened. From February 28 [1026] until the year 1027, this earthquake, that is tremor, seized the region, that is to say the area now called the West—I mean the city of Antioch and the district of Seleucia, *Ksywt,* and the entire seacoast and island[s]. As a result, for this entire time, the inhabitants of villages and cities everywhere made homes and dwelled (along with their remaining livestock) outside their [normal] dwellings, making for themselves tents and huts in fields, mountains, barns, [and] parks. But many others cast their work aside under the open, unprotected air out of fear and terror of that terrible sentence that was brought upon the land and its inhabitants on account of our sins, that is on account of lawlessness.

Then, even as these two terrible afflictions accompanying each other neither ceased nor indeed came to an end, God sent upon the land this third affliction, called plague. Without mercy, innumerable people were buried in various places. And along with this aforementioned affliction, God also sent upon the land a drought and locusts, devastating vineyards, seeds, and plants. All these things were established and done by God for men's providence. Then, along with these, on Saturday, May 20, there was a strong gale of wind such that trees were uprooted, houses collapsed, and men found it hard to stand. Then, after this, there was heavy hail in each and every place, and it pounded the vineyards and plants.

[This occurred] in order that all remaining who had acted wickedly would be corrected by and become afraid of these various, terrifying, terrible, and intolerable afflictions all accompanying one another. [This occurred] so that they would repent for their sins and become terrified of what has been written: Christ, the word of God and the Father, also spoke to the stubborn and hardhearted people of the Jews. "'Do you think,' he said, 'that those upon whom the tower in Siloam collapsed were more sinful than you? Truly I say to you, unless you repent, you will perish like them'" [Lk 13:4–5].

Next, in the year 1026 [715 C.E.], in February, King Walīd died and his brother Sulaymān rose up after him. He judged and subjugated the satraps, chiefs, and money changers under his control. He plundered them and gathered much gold and silver. He even gathered up all the treasures of the Saracens, collected them together, and put them in a treasury in the holy city of Jerusalem, which, as they say, is the center of the earth.

Then, after these things, in the year 1026 [715 C.E.], on April 27, there was rain, or indeed heavy and terrible hail, that also killed many cattle. They drowned in the resulting flood, and people [also] perished in it, as did camels and donkeys. Then, in the year 1027 [716 C.E.], on Monday, April 20, there was a devastating and terrible hail such that plants and seeds were devastated by it, as well as many fowl.

Chronicle ad 724

Miaphysite

ca. 724 C.E.

The *Chronicle ad 724* is one of two surviving Syriac texts from the Umayyad era that provide a list of early caliphs, along with the lengths of their reigns. It begins with a reference to Muḥammad entering Medina and ends with the death of Caliph Yazīd.

Although this particular caliph list survives only in a unique Syriac copy, several factors make it likely that the *Chronicle ad 724* follows an Islamic exemplar. First, as Robert Hoyland points out, an unusual phrase that describes the first year of Muḥammad's reign ("his first year, after he had entered his city and three months before he entered [it]") betrays a strong knowledge of Islamic tradition. Later Muslim writers, such as Muḥammad ibn Jarīr al-Ṭabarī, state that Muḥammad's entry into Medina took place in the third month of the year. This would require A.H. 1 to start three months prior to Muḥammad's emigration, just as it appears in the *Chronicle*'s introduction. Second, as both Hoyland

and Andrew Palmer have noted, the *Chronicle*'s dates correspond with traditional regnal dates only if one uses a lunar calendar, as did early Muslims. The solar calendar that Christians used would make the *Chronicle*'s reigns of individual caliphs, as well as the grand sum appearing in the *Chronicle*'s final line, too long. Finally, the *Chronicle ad 724* contains two Arabic loan words, *rasul* (messenger) and *fitna* (dissension). If it had been originally composed in Syriac, the author most likely would have used Syriac words for these concepts rather than Syriac transliterations of Arabic.

These all suggest that it was not a Christian who originally compiled this list. Rather, a Christian scribe translated an Arabic caliph list, now no longer extant, into Syriac. This work's inclusion in a most likely eighth-century manuscript reminds one how quickly texts crossed confessional and linguistic communities. As a series of textual emendations attest, however, such crossings were not without controversy. The Syriac translator produced a literally faithful translation of the Arabic, for the Syriac repeats its source's traditional claim of Muḥammad being God's *rasul*. The surprise for modern readers is the willingness of an eighth-century Christian to let this stand. In fact, this choice shocked more than just modern readers. At least one ancient reader became so affronted that he erased the word *rasul,* so that only a bit of the *r* remains visible in the extant manuscript.

The *Chronicle ad 724* witnesses what various Christians thought was, and later was not, an acceptable way to refer to Muḥammad. It also preserves important information about early Christian (and most likely earlier Islamic) knowledge about Muslim rulers. For example, like the earlier *Chronicle ad 705*, the *Chronicle ad 724* does not mention the caliph ʿAlī. It instead refers to a five-year-and-four-month period of dissension. So too it does not include the short reign of Muʿāwiya II but instead speaks of nine months of dissension at that time. As a result, this ruler list and its transmission history are particularly valuable for the study of the early caliphate and of early Christian reactions to seventh- and eighth-century political history.

MANUSCRIPT AND EDITIONS

The only surviving copy of *Chronicle ad 724* is preserved in *British Library Additional* 14,643. The first fifty-six pages of this Miaphysite codex contain the *Chronicle ad 640*. The *Chronicle ad 724* immediately follows. A later scribe added some short hymns to the manuscript's end. On paleographic grounds, William Wright estimated the manuscript's composition date as the mid-eighth century. Jan Pieter Nicolaas Land published the first edition of the text in 1862. Ernest Walter Brooks published a new edition in 1904.

AUTHORSHIP AND DATE OF COMPOSITION

The *Chronicle ad 724* ends with Caliph Yazīd's death in 724. It was thus written after 724 and most likely before the death of Yazīd's successor, Caliph Hishām, in 743. Because it never mentions Hishām's reign, several scholars have suggested that the *Chronicle* was originally composed in the mid-720s, soon after Yazīd's death. If Wright's paleographic judgment is correct and *British Library Additional* 14,643 was written in the mid-eighth century, the surviving manuscript copy dates to within a few decades of the *Chronicle*'s composition.

.   .   .

A notice concerning the life of Muḥammad, the messenger of God—from his first year, after he had entered his city and three months before he entered [it]; and how long each subsequent king who rose up over the Hagarenes lived after they began to reign; and how long there was dissension among them.

Three months before Muḥammad came.

And Muḥammad lived ten [more] years.

Abū Bakr, son of Abū Quḥāfa: two years and six months.

'Umar, son of al-Khaṭṭab: ten years and three months.

'Uthmān, son of 'Affān: twelve years.

After 'Uthmān, dissension: five years and four months.

Mu'āwiya, son of Abū Sufyān: nineteen years and two months.

Yazīd, son of Mu'āwiya: three years and eight months.

After Yazīd, dissension: nine months.

Marwān, son of al-Ḥakam: nine months.

'Abd al-Malik, son of Marwān: twenty-one years and one month.

Walīd, son of 'Abd al-Malik: nine years and eight months.

Sulaymān, son of 'Abd al-Malik: two years and nine months.

'Umar, son of 'Abd al-Azīz: two years and five months.

Yazīd, son of 'Abd al-Malik: four years, one month, and two days.

All the years come to one hundred and four, five months, and two days.

Disputation of John
and the Emir

Miaphysite

Most likely early eighth century C.E.

The *Disputation of John and the Emir* relates an alleged conversation between the seventh-century Miaphysite patriarch of Antioch John Sedra and an unspecified Muslim leader. The text purports to be a letter written by an unnamed companion of the patriarch. In order to reassure the reader of John's safety, the narrator describes how the patriarch had a friendly audience with the Muslim official.

The majority of the text consists of a dialogue between John and the emir. The emir presents a series of brief questions, and John gives more lengthy responses. They discuss topics such as the diversity of Christian beliefs, Christ's divinity, who was controlling the world when Christ was in Mary's womb, why the Hebrew prophets did not explicitly speak of Jesus, and what laws Christians follow. The narrative interrupts this pattern of question and answer only once, in order that the emir might summon a Jew to confirm John's scriptural citations.

After relating the dialogue, the narrator states that even the Chalcedonian Christians present prayed for John, as they knew that the Miaphysite patriarch was representing all Christians before the emir. The text also asks the reader to pray that God will enlighten the emir and make him favorably disposed toward Christians. The work ends with a list of other people whom the narrator wants the letter's readers to support in prayer.

Recent scholarship suggests that it is very unlikely that a Miaphysite patriarch and a Muslim official ever exchanged the words preserved in this text. Nevertheless, *John and the Emir* remains an important witness to what early Syriac Christians imagined such encounters might be like. Even if more likely written in the early eighth century than in the early seventh, the *Disputation* reflects what its contemporaries considered some of the most pressing theological issues brought about by the rise of Islam. Like most disputation texts, *John and the Emir* is not so much an attempt at objective historiography as an act of apologetics, polemic, and self-representation.

MANUSCRIPT AND EDITIONS

In 874 a monk named Abraham composed a ninety-nine-folio manuscript now housed in the British Library (*BL Add.* 17,193). He titled his work "A volume of demonstrations, collections, and letters" and included in it more than 125 short pieces ranging from biblical passages and excerpts from church fathers to lists of councils, caliphs, and calamities. Following a canon of Severus of Antioch regarding baptism and preceding a list of eighth-century disasters are three folios that make up the sole witness to *John and the Emir*. Fraçois Nau published an edition of this text in 1915. Michael Penn published a revised edition in 2008.

AUTHORSHIP AND DATE OF COMPOSITION

Dionysius of Tel Maḥrē (d. 845) speaks of a Muslim emir, Bar Sa'd, summoning the patriarch John of Antioch for an audience. Impressed by John's answers to his questions, the emir commanded him to have the Gospel translated into Arabic. Although it was composed almost two centuries after John's death, many scholars use this reference to argue that the Miaphysite author of *John and the Emir* wrote shortly after a real encounter between the patriarch and an Arab notable, most likely 'Umayr ibn Sa'd al-Anṣāri.

According to *John and the Emir*, this meeting took place on Sunday, May 9. There were three years during John's tenure as patriarch (r. 631–48) when May 9 fell on a Sunday: 633, 639, and 644. If written soon after any of these dates, *John and the Emir* would be the earliest witness to an interfaith dialogue between Christians and Muslims. But even if this were the case, the selective nature of the discussed topics, the characterization of the patriarch and his Muslim interlocutor, and the presence of numerous apologetic motifs make it quite clear that this document would still be far from an accurate transcript of John and the emir's discussion.

Other scholars, however, see *John and the Emir* as a literary production written decades after John's death in order to serve the needs of an eighth-century Miaphysite community. Several arguments support this later dating of the text. Details in Dionysius of Tel Maḥrē's account appear dependent on *John and the Emir*, calling into question the historical basis for the described encounter. *John and the Emir*'s silence regarding the emir's identity, title, and location, as well as any information about the letter's recipients, seems surprising for a contemporary witness. The text's concerns for Islam's claim as an independent religious tradition and questions regarding inheritance law fit much better with our knowledge of eighth-century Syriac Christianity than with a mid-seventh century context. The style, the content, and even the term *Hagarene* show much greater affinities with eighth-century Syriac texts, such as the *Disputation of Bēt Halē*, than with seventh-century works.

The sole manuscript preserving the *Disputation of John and the Emir* includes a colophon dated to 874, and it remains possible that *John and the Emir* could have been written as recently as the last decades of the ninth century. Although such a late date cannot definitely be ruled out, *John and the Emir*'s depiction of Islam seems substantially less developed and detailed than those found in most Abbasid-era texts, and the majority of recent scholars suggest a composition date during the first half of the eighth century.

.   .   .

Next, the letter of Mār John the patriarch concerning the conversation that he had with the emir of the Hagarenes.

Because we know that you are anxious and afraid on our behalf due to the affair for which we have been called to this region [along with] the blessed and God-honored father, lord, and patriarch of ours—we inform your love that on the ninth of this month of May, on holy Sunday, we entered before the glorious commander, the emir. The blessed one and father of all was asked by him if the gospel that all those in the entire world who are and are called Christians hold is one and the same and does not vary in anything. The blessed one answered him, "It is one and the same to the Greeks, the Romans, the Syrians, the Egyptians, the Ethiopians, the Indians, the Aramaeans, the Persians, and the rest of all peoples and languages."

He also inquired, "Why, when the gospel is one, is the faith diverse?" The blessed one answered, "Just as the Torah is one and the same and is accepted by us Christians, by you Hagarenes, by the Jews, and by the Samaritans, but each people differs in faith, so also concerning the gospel's faith: each sect understands and interprets it differently, and not like us."

He also inquired, "What do you say Christ is? Is he God or not?" Our father answered, "He is God and the Word that was born from God the Father, eternally and without beginning. At the end of times, for men's salvation, he took flesh and became incarnate from the Holy Spirit and from Mary—the holy one and the Virgin, the mother of God—and he became man."

87 The glorious emir also asked him, "When Christ, who you say is God, was in Mary's womb, who bore and governed the heavens and the earth?" Our blessed father immediately replied, "When God descended to Mount Sinai and was there speaking with Moses for forty days and forty nights, who bore and governed the heavens and the earth? For you say that you accept Moses and his books." The emir said, "It was God, and he governed the heavens and the earth." Immediately he heard from our father, "Thus Christ [is] God; when he was in the womb of the Virgin, as almighty God he bore and governed the heavens, the earth, and everything in them."

The glorious emir also said, "As for Abraham and Moses, what sort of faith and belief did they have?" Our blessed father said, "Abraham, Isaac, Jacob, Moses, Aaron, and the rest of the prophets and all the just and righteous ones had and held the faith and belief of Christians." The emir said, "Why then did they not write openly and make [it] known concerning Christ?" Our blessed father answered, "As [God's] confidants and intimates they knew. But [there was] the childishness and uneducated state of the people at that time who were inclined and attracted toward a multitude of gods to the point of considering even pieces of wood, stones, and many things [to be] gods and erecting idols, worshiping them, and sacrificing to them. The holy ones did not want to give the errant an occasion to depart from the living God and to go after error. But cautiously they said that which is the truth: 'Hear, Israel, that the Lord your God, the Lord is one' [Dt 6:5]. For they truly knew that God is one and [that there is] one divinity of the Father and of the Son and of the Holy Spirit. Because of this, they spoke and wrote secretly concerning God, that he is one and the same in divinity and is three hypostases and persons. But he is not, nor is he confessed [to be], three gods or three divinities or, by any means, gods and divinities. Because [there is] one divinity of the Father, the Son, and the Holy Spirit, as we have said. And from the Father are the Son and the Spirit. If you want, I am willing and ready to confirm all these things from the holy scriptures."

88

After the emir also heard these things, he asked only that if Christ is God and was born from Mary and if God has a son that it immediately be shown to him also from the Torah. The blessed one said, "Not only Moses but also all the holy prophets prophesized beforehand and wrote these things concerning Christ. One wrote concerning his birth from a virgin, another that he would be born in Bethlehem, another concerning his baptism. All of them, so to say, [wrote] concerning his salvific suffering, his life-giving death, and his glorious resurrection from among the dead after three days." And he immediately brought forth examples and began to confirm [these things] from all the prophets and from Moses.

But the glorious emir did not accept these things from the prophets but wanted it to be shown to him [from] Moses that Christ is God. The same blessed one, along with many other [passages], brought forth this [one from] Moses: "The Lord brought down from before the Lord fire and sulfur upon Sodom and upon Gomorrah" [Gn 19:24]. The glorious emir asked that this be shown in the scripture. Without delay our father showed [this] in the full Greek and Syriac scriptures. For in [that] place there were also present with us certain Hagarenes. And they saw with their eyes those writings and the glorious name of "the Lord" and "the Lord." Indeed, the emir summoned a Jewish man who was [there] and was considered by them an expert of scripture. He asked him if this was so in the wording in the Torah. But he answered, "I do not know exactly."

From here the emir moved to asking about the laws of the Christians, what and what sort [of laws] they are and whether they are written in the gospel. He also [asked], "If a man dies and leaves sons or daughters, a wife, a mother, a sister, and a cousin, how should his property be divided among them?" And after our holy father said, "The gospel is divine, for it teaches and commands the heavenly teachings and life-giving commandments and rejects all sins and evils and through itself teaches virtue and righteousness," many things were discussed regarding this subject—while there were gathered there [many] people, not only nobles of the Hagarenes but also chiefs and leaders of cities and of believing and Christ-loving people: the Tanukāyē and Tuʿāyē and the ʿAqulāyē.

And the glorious emir said, "I want you to do one of three [things]: either show me that your laws are written in the gospel and be guided by them or submit to the Hagarene law." When our father answered, "We Christians have laws that are just, are upright, and agree with the teaching and commandments of the gospel, the canons of the apostles, and the laws of the church," that first day's assembly was thus concluded. And we have not yet come to enter before him again.

It was commanded by him that some people from the bishoprics of the Council of Chalcedon also come. Indeed, everyone who was present [both] from the Orthodox and from the Chalcedonians prayed for the life and safety of the blessed lord patriarch. They glorified and magnified God, who generously provided the word of truth for his eloquence and filled him with the power and grace which is from him, according to his true promises when he said, "They will stand you before kings and governors on account of me. But do not worry what you will say and be not concerned. At that hour, what you should say will be given to you. For you will not speak. Rather the spirit of your Father will speak through you" [Lk 12:11–12].

We have reported to your love these few of the many things that were very recently discussed so that you might diligently and continually pray for us without ceasing and entreat the Lord that he, in his mercy, care for his church and his people and that Christ make a resolution to this affair that pleases his will, aids his church, and comforts his people. For, as we said above, also those of the Council of Chalcedon prayed for the blessed Mār patriarch, because he spoke on behalf of the entire Christian community and did not speak against them. They continually communicated with him and sought his blessedness to thus speak on behalf of the entire community and not to stir up anything against them. For they knew their weakness and the greatness of the danger and anguish that awaited if the Lord did not care for his church in accord with his mercy.

Pray for the glorious emir, that God would enlighten and instruct him concerning what is pleasing to the Lord and is beneficial. The blessed father of all, the revered fathers with him—Abba Mār Thomas, Mār Severus, Mār Sergius, Mār Aitilaha, Mār John, and their entire holy synodal board—as well as the leaders and believers who are gathered here with us, especially our beloved Mār Andrew (both a wise leader and one guarded by Christ), and we [who are] least in the Lord ask for your peace and holy prayers always.

Exegetical Homilies

MĀR ABBĀ II

East Syrian

Late seventh to mid-eighth century C.E.

When he died in 751, the East Syrian catholicos Mār Abbā II of Kashkar was reputedly 110 years old. He wrote a large number of works, which, for the most part, no longer survive. A later medieval compilation, however, preserves fragments from his *Exegetical Homilies* that document early Muslim knowledge of the New Testament and early Christian knowledge of the Qur'an.

The most explicit reference occurs in a discussion of John 20:17 explicitly attributed to Mār Abbā II. Here he complains that the "Arabians of our time" are using Jesus's statement in the Gospel of John that he ascends "to my God and your God" as proof that Jesus is not divine. A slightly longer passage that also most likely comes from Mār Abbā is more circumspect. It discusses the commemoration of Mary in Matthew 1:18–25 and includes an enigmatic polemic against those who deny Christ's birth. Gerrit Reinink's careful analysis of the passage shows that this too is almost certainly a reference to Muslims' rejection of Christ's divinity. Its mention of a creed that does not accept the term *birth* may be the earliest Christian allusion to the statement in the Qur'an's surah 112 that God neither begets nor is begotten.

MANUSCRIPTS AND EDITION

Excerpts from Mār Abbā are now found in the *Gannat Bussāmē* (Garden of Delights), a commentary on the East Syrian lectionary most likely compiled between the tenth and thirteenth centuries. A number of manuscripts preserve the *Gannat Bussāmē*, but there is no critical edition of the entire work. In 1999 Gerrit Reinink published a translation of the first passage and a transliteration and translation of the second as it appears in *Urmia* 180, a manuscript dated on paleographic grounds to the fourteenth or fifteenth century and now held at Princeton Theological Seminary.

AUTHORSHIP AND DATE OF COMPOSITION

The *Gannat Bussāmē* presents the passage translated below without attribution. As Reinink has pointed out, however, it is in a part of the work that often quotes Mār Abbā, sometimes by name and sometimes anonymously. Additionally, its topic and style are extremely similar to those of quotations explicitly attributed to him. The previous sentence refers to Mary's perpetual virginity, a topic that an earlier quotation from Mār Abbā, on Matthew 1:25, also addresses. So too the passage contains several rhetorical flourishes that are quite typical of Mār Abbā's writings, such as the wordplay between *erased* (Syriac root: *lḥw*) and *lick* (Syriac root: *lḥk*) and between *column* (Syriac root: *gwr*) and *company* (Syriac root: *gwd*; in Syriac, *d* and *r* have the same letterform, distinguished only by a dot). No one has questioned Reinink's conclusion. It is not known, however, when Mār Abbā wrote his *Exegetical Homilies*. Any time in the late seventh century up to his death in 751 remains possible.

.　　.　　.

You have seen how much the ages—I mean yours—have rushed in and flourished, recently [becoming] cutters of "forever" from "and [Joseph] did not know her" [Mt 1:25]. Also remind yourself of their great misfortune. For [while] they erased "birth" from the column of a page, the Lord will lick the deniers from the company of the living. For they do not accept "birth" in their creed.

Disputation of Bēt Ḥalē

East Syrian

Most likely early to mid-eighth century C.E.

A soon to be published text with the manuscript title *The Disputation That Took Place between an Arab Notable and a Monk in the Monastery of Bēt Ḥalē* provides particularly important data for assessing early Syriac reactions to the rise of Islam. Scholars use a variety of shorter titles to refer to this document, such as *Disputation of Bēt Ḥalē*. If scholarly consensus is correct and this anonymous East Syrian text was composed around the 720s, it is one of the earliest surviving Christian disputation texts concerning Islam and the first to explicitly speak of the Qur'an.

After a brief prologue, the text presents a short first-person narrative stating that an Arab notable who served the governor Maslama had become sick, visited the narrator's monastery, and stayed there for ten days. Having knowledge of both Christian scripture and the Qur'an, he began to challenge the narrator regarding Christian practices and beliefs. The remainder of the text uses a question-and-answer format alternating between quotes attributed to "the Arab" and quotes attributed to "the monk."

The resulting eight-folio discussion between these interlocutors concerns topics such as the geographical extent of the Islamic conquests, circumcision, typological exegesis, Trinitarian theology, Christology, Muḥammad, Christian veneration of relics, Christians praying to the East, soteriology, and the origins of the Qur'an. This supposed transcript ends with the Arab declaring that were it not for the fear of repercussions, many Arabs would convert to Christianity. Because David Taylor is soon publishing an edition and translation of this text soon, I have not here provided my own translation.

MANUSCRIPTS AND EDITION

The *Disputation of Bēt Ḥalē* appears in at least two extant manuscripts, *Diyarbekir 95*, dated to the early eighteenth century, and *Mardin 82*, composed in 1890. Another copy was found in *Siirt 112*, which was dated on paleographic grounds to the fifteenth century but was most likely destroyed soon after World War I. The text may also appear in *Alqosh, Notre-Dame des Semences 144*, dated on paleographic grounds to the nineteenth century. However, this manuscript's inaccessibility to scholars has prevented any from verifying that what an earlier cataloger described simply as a disputation between an Arab and a monk is indeed the *Disputation of Bēt Ḥalē*.

For some time, photographs of the Diyarbekir manuscript have circulated among scholars, and translated excerpts from the majority of the text are scattered throughout a number of published articles. David Taylor has produced and privately circulated his edition and English translation of the Diyarbekir version of the text, which will be published shortly.

AUTHORSHIP AND DATE OF COMPOSITION

The *Disputation of Bēt Ḥalē* claims to have been written by an anonymous monk at the monastery of Bēt Ḥalē who conversed with a visiting Arab official. Additional authorial information may come from the catalogue of 'Abdisho of Nisibis (d. 1318), which speaks of a disputation against the Arabs written by Abraham of Bēt Ḥalē, who was most likely an early eighth-century pupil of the bishop of Ḥīra John Azraq. Nevertheless, it cannot be determined whether 'Abdisho's claim is correct or whether he simply repeated a later attribution of an originally anonymous text.

Although it remains possible that the text reflects some sort of historical encounter between a monk and an Arab, in its current form the *Disputation of Bēt Ḥalē* is a carefully constructed literary text. Both the Arab's constant agreement with the monk's statements and his final concession that Christian doctrine is superior to that of the Arabs demonstrate that it is much more interested in apologetics and polemics than in providing a transcript of an actual interfaith encounter.

Nevertheless, two narrative details may help establish the work's provenance. The first is the physical setting, the East Syrian monastery of Bēt Ḥalē. There are two East Syrian monasteries known by that name, one near Mosul, in northern Mesopotamia, and the other near Ḥīra, in southern Iraq. Because neither was particularly prominent, the author would have had little reason to set the narrative there besides being in a region with a monastery named Bēt Ḥalē.

The second detail regards the temporal setting. At the text's beginning, the narrator states that the visiting Arab served the governor Maslama. The reference is most likely to the son of the Umayyad caliph 'Abd al-Malik. This Maslama died in 738 and had jurisdiction over the monastery of Bēt Ḥalē near Mosul beginning in 710 but over the one near Ḥīra only from 720 to 721, while he was briefly governor of that area as well. Of course, the story's being set in the early seventh century does not necessarily mean that it was composed then. But a later author who wanted to pass off a text as being written substantially earlier than it really was most likely would have alluded to a much more historically prominent individual than Maslama, a figure whom Christians were unlikely to have commonly remembered decades, not to say centuries, after his death. So too, if the author wanted the temporal setting to add authority to his writing, he most likely would have chosen the earliest period of Christian-Muslim encounters, just as the author of the *Disputation of John and the Emir* had. Since the author of the *Disputation of Bēt Ḥalē* did neither, most see the allusion to Maslama as evidence that the text was written not too long after Maslama's governorship. Further support for an Umayyad-period composition date can be found in the author's apparent knowledge of Islam, which is much less detailed than that of most Abbasid-era Syriac texts. As a result, most scholars conclude that the *Disputation of Bēt Ḥalē* was written after 710 but most likely before the Abbasid revolution.

BIBLIOGRAPHY

ABBREVIATIONS

Christian-Muslim Relations	*Christian-Muslim Relations: A Bibliographic History*, vol. 1, *600–900*, edited by David Thomas and Barbara Roggema (Leiden: Brill, 2009)
CSCO	*Corpus scriptorum christianorum orientalium* (1904–present)
EDSH	*Encyclopedic Dictionary of the Syriac Heritage*, edited by Aaron Butts, Sebastian Brock, George Kiraz, and Lucas Van Rompay (Piscataway, NJ: Gorgias Press, 2011)
Hoyland, *Seeing Islam*	Robert G. Hoyland, *Seeing Islam as Others Saw It: A Survey and Evaluation of Christian, Jewish and Zoroastrian Writings on Early Islam* (Princeton: Darwin Press, 1997)
Palmer, *West-Syrian Chronicles*	Andrew Palmer, *The Seventh Century in the West-Syrian Chronicles* (Liverpool: Liverpool University Press, 1993)

Suermann, *Die geschichtstheologische Reaktion*	Harald Suermann, *Die geschichtstheologische Reaktion auf die einfallenden Muslime in der edessenischen Apokalyptik des 7. Jahrhunderts* (New York: P. Lang, 1985)
Wright, *Catalogue*	William Wright, *Catalogue of Syriac Manuscripts in the British Museum Acquired since the Year 1838*, vols. 1–3 (London: Longman, 1870–72)

PROLOGUE

The concluding quotation is from *Chronicle ad 1234* (edition in *CSCO* 81: 251; translation my own).

For works on Heraclius and his campaigns, see especially James Howard-Johnston, *Witnesses to a World Crisis: Historians and Histories of the Middle East in the Seventh Century* (Oxford: Oxford University Press, 2010); Walter Emil Kaegi, *Heraclius: Emperor of Byzantium* (Cambridge: Cambridge University Press, 2003).

For Christological controversies, the standard reference remains Alois Grillmeier's four-volume *Jesus der Christus im Glauben der Kirche* (Freiburg im Breisgau: Herder, 1979–90). For some more recent (and concise) discussions that focus on the controversies' impact on Syriac Christianity, see especially Wilhelm Baum and Dietmar W. Winkler, *Die apostolische Kirche des Ostens: Geschichte der sogenannten Nestorianer* (Klagenfurt: Verlag Kitab, 2000), 25–34; S.P. Brock, "The 'Nestorian' Church: A Lamentable Misnomer," *Bulletin of the John Rylands Library of Manchester* 78, no. 3 (1996): 32–35; Adam M. Schor, *Theodoret's People: Social Networks and Religious Conflict in Late Roman Syria* (Berkeley: University of California Press, 2011), 3–5; Lucas Van Rompay, "The East (3): Syria and Mesopotamia," in *The Oxford Handbook of Early Christian Studies,* edited by Susan Ashbrook Harvey and David G. Hunter (Oxford: Oxford University Press, 2008), 376–78; Van Rompay, "Society and Community in the Christian East," in *The Cambridge Companion to the Age of Justinian,* edited by Michael Maas (Cambridge: Cambridge University Press, 2004), 239–66.

For overviews of the Islamic conquests, see Fred McGraw Donner, *Early Islamic Conquests* (Princeton: Princeton University Press, 1981); Donner, "The Islamic Conquests," in *A Companion to the History of the Middle East,* edited by Youssef M. Choueiri (Malden, MA: Blackwell Publishing, 2005), 28–51; Walter E. Kaegi, *Byzantium and the Early Islamic Conquests* (Cambridge: Cambridge University Press, 1992).

INTRODUCTION

For a more in-depth discussion of Syriac Christian reactions to Islam, see especially Michael Philip Penn, *Envisioning Islam: Syriac Christians in the Early Muslim World* (Pennsylvania: University of Pennsylvania Press, 2015).

For general works on the Umayyad dynasty, see especially Fred M. Donner, *Muhammad and the Believers: At the Origins of Islam* (Cambridge, MA: Harvard University Press, 2010); Gerald R. Hawting, *The First Dynasty of Islam: The Umayyad Caliphate, AD 661–750,* 2nd ed. (New York: Routledge, 2000); Hugh Kennedy, *The Prophet and the Age of the Caliphates: The Islamic Near East from the Sixth to the Eleventh Century* (New York: Longman Publishing, 1986); Chase F. Robinson, *'Abd al-Malik* (Oxford: Oneworld, 2005); Robinson, "The Rise of Islam, 600–705," in *The New Cambridge History of Islam: The Formation of the Islamic World, Sixth to Eleventh Centuries,* edited by Robinson (Cambridge: Cambridge University Press, 2010), 173–225.

ACCOUNT OF 637

CSCO 2: 75 [edition]; *CSCO* 4: 60 [Latin translation]; Hoyland, *Seeing Islam,* 116–17; Theodor Nöldeke, "Zur Geschichte der Araber im 1. Jahrh. d.H. aus syrischen Quellen," *Zeitschrift der Deutschen Morgenländischen Gesellschaft* 29 (1875): 76–82 [edition and German translation]; Palmer, *West Syrian Chronicles,* 1–4 [English translation]; Michael Philip Penn, "Monks, Manuscripts, and Muslims: Syriac Textual Changes in Reaction to the Rise of Islam," *Hugoye: Journal of Syriac Studies* 12, no. 2 (2009): 240; Jack Tannous, "Account of the Subjugation of Syria by the

Arabs," at www.doaks.org (Dumbarton Oaks website) [English translation]; Wright, *Catalogue* 1:65–66.

CHRONICLE AD 640

CSCO 2: 76–154 [edition]; *CSCO* 5: 76–154 [Latin translation]; James Howard-Johnston, *Witnesses to a World Crisis: Historians and Histories of the Middle East in the Seventh Century* (Oxford: Oxford University Press, 2010), 59–66; Hoyland, *Seeing Islam*, 118–20; Andrew Palmer, "Une chronique syriaque contemporaine de la conquête arabe: Essai d'interprétation théologique et politique," in *La Syrie de Byzance à l'Islam, VIIe–VIIIe Siècles*, edited by Pierre Canivet and Jean-Paul Rey-Coquais (Damascus: Institut Français de Damas, 1992), 331–46; Palmer, *West-Syrian Chronicles*, 5–24 [English translation]; Wright, *Catalogue* 3:1040–41.

LETTERS, ISHO'YAHB III

The scholarship on Isho'yahb III is quite large. The most thorough bibliography can be found in Ovidiu Ioan, *Muslime und Araber bei Īshō'jahb III. (649–659)* (Wiesbaden: Harrassowitz, 2009). Scholarship that focuses on Isho'yahb's references to Islam includes *Christian-Muslim Relations*, 133–36; *CSCO* 11: 93–97, 247–55, 262–70 [edition]; *CSCO* 12: 93–97, 247–55, 262–70 [Latin translation]; *EDSH*, 179; Victoria L. Erhart, "The Church of the East during the Period of the Four Rightly-Guided Caliphs," *Bulletin of the John Rylands Library of Manchester* 78 (1996): 55–71; John F. Healey, "The Christians of Qatar in the 7th Century A.D.," in *Studies in Honour of Clifford Edmund Bosworth*, edited by Clifford Edmund Bosworth and Ian Richard Netton (Leiden: Brill, 2000), 222–37; Healey, "The Patriarch Išo'yabh III and the Christians of Qatar in the First Islamic Century," in *The Christian Heritage of Iraq: Collected Papers from the Christianity in Iraq Seminar Days, 2004–2008*, edited by Erica C.D. Hunter (Piscataway, NJ: Gorgias Press, 2009), 1–9; Hoyland, *Seeing Islam*, 174–82; Ioan, "Arabien und die Araber im kirchenleitenden Handeln des Katholikos Patriarchen Ischo'jahb III. (649–659)," in *Die Suryoye und ihre Umwelt: 4. deutsches Syrologen-Symposium in Trier 2004—Festgabe Wolfgang Hage zum 70. Geburtstag*, edited by Martin Tamcke and Andreas Heinz, 43–58 (Münster: Lit, 2005); Ioan, *Muslime und Araber bei Īshō'jahb III. (649–659)* (Wiesbaden: Harrassowitz, 2009), 89–122; Richard E. Payne, "Persecuting Heresy in Early Islamic Iraq: The Catholicos Ishoyahb III and the Elites of Nisibis," in *The Power of Religion in Antiquity*, edited by Andrew Cain and Noel Lenski (Burlington, VT: Ashgate, 2009), 397–409; Martin Tamcke, "The Catholicos Isho'jahb III and Giwargis and the Arabs," in *Les Syriaques transmetteurs de civilisations: L'Expérience du Bilād El-Shām à l'époque omeyyade*, edited by Markaz al-Abḥāth wa-al-Dirāsāt al-Mashriqīyah Mu'tamar al-Turāth al-Suryānī and al-Jāmi'ah al-Anṭūnīyah Markaz al-Dirāsāt wa-al-Abḥ āth al-Mashriqīyah (Antélias, Lebanon: Centre d'Études et de Recherches Orientales, 2005), 201–9; William G. Young, *Patriarch, Shah and Caliph: A Study of the Relationships of the Church of the East with the Sassanid Empire and the Early Caliphates up to 820 AD* (Rawalpindi: Christian Study Centre, 1974), 85–99.

APOCALYPSE OF PSEUDO-EPHREM

Christian-Muslim Relations, 160–62; CSCO 320: 60–71 [edition]; CSCO 321: 79–84 [German translation]; Hoyland, *Seeing Islam*, 260–63; G. J. Reinink, "Alexander the Great in Seventh-Century Syriac 'Apocalyptic' Texts," in *The Acts of Alexander the Great: The Unique Monument of Medieval Toreutics Found in the Village Muzhi of Yamal-Nenetz Autonomic District*, vol. 2, edited by S. S. Akentiev (Saint Petersburg: Byzantinorossica, 2003), 169–71; Reinink, "Pseudo-Ephraems 'Rede über das Ende' und die syrische eschatologische Literatur des siebenten Jahrhunderts," *ARAM* 5 (1993): 437–63; Suermann, *Die geschichtstheologische Reaktion*, 12–33, 111–29 [edition and German translation]; Jeffrey Thomas Wickes, "Time, Wickedness and Identity in Pseudo-Ephrem's Homily on the End" (MA thesis, Notre Dame, 2007) [includes English translation].

KHUZISTAN CHRONICLE

Christian-Muslim Relations, 130–32; CSCO 1: 15–39 [edition]; CSCO 2: 15–32 [Latin translation]; James Howard-Johnston, *Witnesses to a World Crisis: Historians and Histories of the Middle East in the Seventh Century* (Oxford:

Oxford University Press, 2010), 128–35; Hoyland, *Seeing Islam*, 182–89; Florence Jullien, "La chronique du Ḫūzistān: Une page d'histoire sassanide," in *Trésors d'Orient: Mélanges offerts à Rika Gyselen*, edited by Philippe Gignoux, Christelle Jullien, and Florence Jullien (Paris: Association pour l'avancement des études iraniennes, 2010), 159–86 [French transl.]; Pierre Nautin, "L'Auteur de la 'Chronique anonyme du Guidi': Élie de Merw," *Revue de l'histoire des religions* 199 (1982): 303–13; Theodor Nöldeke, "Die von Guidi herausgegebene syrische Chronik übersetzt und commentiert," in *Sitzungeberichte der Kaiserlichen Akademie der Wissenschaften philosophisch-historische Klasse 128* (Vienna: Tempsky, 1893), 1–48 [German translation]; Chase F. Robinson, "The Conquest of Khūzistān: A Historigraphical Reassessment," *Bulletin of SOAS* 67, no. 1 (2004): 14–39.

MARONITE CHRONICLE

M. Breydy, "Das Chronikon des Maroniten Theophilus ibn Tuma," *Journal of Oriental and Afircan Studies* 2 (1990): 34–46; Breydy, *Geschichte der syro-arabischen Literatur der Maroniten vom VII. bis XVI. Jahrhundert* (Opladen: Westdeutscher, 1985), 130–38; *Christian-Muslim Relations*, 145–47; *CSCO* 3: 43–74 [edition]; *CSCO* 4: 37–57 [Latin translation]; James Howard-Johnson, *Witnesses to a World Crisis: Historians and Histories of the Middle East in the Seventh Century* (Oxford: Oxford University Press, 2010), 175–78; Hoyland, *Seeing Islam*, 135–39; François Nau, "Opuscules Maronites," *Revue de l'Orient Chrétien* 4 (1899): 322–28; Theodor Nöldeke, "Zur Geschichte der Araber im 1. Jahrh. d.H. aus syrischen Quellen," *Zeitschrift der Deutschen Morgenländischen Gesellschaft* 29 (1875): 82–98; Palmer, *West-Syrian Chronicles*, 29–35 [English translation]; Wright, *Catalogue* 3:1041.

SYRIAC LIFE OF MAXIMUS THE CONFESSOR

Sebastian Brock, "An Early Syriac Life of Maximus the Confessor," *Analecta Bollandiana* 91 (1973): 299–346 [edition and English translation], reprinted in Brock, *Syriac Perspectives on Late Antiquity* (London: Variorum Reprints, 1984), 299–346; Hoyland, *Seeing Islam*, 139–42; Wright, *Catalogue* 3:1206.

CANONS, GEORGE I

Oscar Braun, *Das Buch der Synhados nach einer Handschrift des Museo Borgiano* (Stuttgart: J. Roth, 1900), 333–48; J.-B. Chabot, *Synodicon orientale ou recueil de synodes nestoriens* (Paris: Imprimerie Nationale, 1902), 215–26 [edition], 480–90 [French translation]; *Christian-Muslim Relations,* 88–89, 151–53; *EDSH, 175;* Hoyland, *Seeing Islam,* 192–94; Uriel I. Simonsohn, *A Common Justice: The Legal Allegiances of Christians and Jews under Early Islam* (Philadelphia: University of Pennsylvania Press, 2011), 103.

COLOPHON OF *BRITISH LIBRARY ADDITIONAL* 14,666

Sebastian Brock, "The Use of Hijra Dating in Syriac Manuscripts: A Preliminary Investigation," in *Redefining Christian Identity: Cultural Interaction in the Middle East since the Rise of Islam,* edited by J.J. van Ginkel, H.L. Murre-van den Berg, and T.M. van Lint (Leuven: Peeters, 2005), 278, 283; William Henry Paine Hatch, *An Album of Dated Syriac Manuscripts* (Boston: American Academy of Arts and Sciences, 1946), 94–95; Wright, *Catalogue* 1:92.

LETTER, ATHANASIUS OF BALAD

Christian-Muslim Relations, 157–59; *CSCO* Subsidia 35: 200–202; Rifaat Y. Ebied, "The Syriac Encyclical Letter of Athanasius II, Patriarch of Antioch, Which Forbids the Partaking of the Sacrifices of the Muslims," in *Orientalia Christiana: Festschrift für Hubert Kaufhold zum 70. Geburtstag,* edited by Peter Bruns and Heinz Otto Luthe (Wiesbaden: Harrassowitz Verlag, 2013), 169–74 [edition and English translation]; *EDSH,* 46; Hoyland, *Seeing Islam,* 147–48; François Nau, "Littérature canonique syriaque inédite," *Revue de l'Orient Chrétien* 14 (1909): 128–30 [edition and French translation]; Michael Philip Penn, "Monks, Manuscripts, and Muslims: Syriac Textual Changes in Reaction to the Rise of Islam," *Hugoye: Journal of Syriac Studies* 12, no. 2 (2009): 244–46.

BOOK OF MAIN POINTS, JOHN BAR PENKĀYĒ

M. Albert, "Une centurie de Mar Jean bar Penkayē," in *Mélanges Antoine Guillaumont* (Geneva: Patrick Cramer, 1988), 143–51; Sebastian Brock, "North Mesopotamia in the Late Seventh Century: Book XV of John Bar Penkāyē's *Rīš Mellē*," *Jerusalem Studies in Arabic and Islam* 9 (1987): 51–74 [English translation]; Peter Bruns, "Von Adam und Eva bis Mohammed—Beobachtungen zur syrischen Chronik des Johannes bar Penkaye," *Oriens Christianus* 87 (2003): 47–64; *Christian-Muslim Relations*, 176–81; *EDSH*, 440; Hoyland, *Seeing Islam*, 194–200; T. Jansma, "Projet d'edition du Ketaba d-rēshmellē, de Jean bar Penkayē," *L'Orient syrien* 8 (1963): 87–106; Herbert Kaufhold, "Anmerkungen zur Textüberlieferung der Chronik des Johannes bar Penkāyē," *Oriens Christianus* 87 (2003): 65–79; Alphonse Mingana, *Sources syriaques I* (Leipzig: Dominican Press, 1907), *1–*171, 172–97 [edition and French translation]; K. Pinggéra, "Nestorianische Weltchronistik: Johannes Bar Penkāyē und Elias von Nisibis," in *Julius Africanus und die christliche Weltchronik,* edited by M. Wallraff (Berlin: Walter de Gruyter, 2005), 263–83; Gerrit J. Reinink, "East Syrian Historiography in Response to the Rise of Islam: The Case of John Bar Penkaye's Ktābā d-rēš mellē," in *Redefining Christian Identity: Cultural Interaction in the Middle East since the Rise of Islam,* edited by J.J. van Ginkel, H.L. Murre-van den Berg, and T.M. van Lint (Leuven: Peeters, 2005), 77–90; Reinink, "Paideia: God's Design in World History According to the East Syrian Monk John bar Penkaye," in *The Medieval Chronicle II: Proceedings of the 2nd International Conference on the Medieval Chronicle Driebergen/Utrecht 16–21 July 1999,* edited by Erik Kooper (Amsterdam: Rodopi, 2002), 190–98; Addai Scher, "Notice sur la vie et les oeuvres de Yohannan bar Penkaye," *Journal Asiatique* 10 (1907): 161–78; Jean-Louis Simonet, "Les citations des Actes des Apôtres dans les chapitres édités du *Ketaba deres melle* de Jean Bar Penkaye," *Le Muséon* 114 (2001): 97–119; Harald Suermann, "Das Arabische Reich in der Weltgeschichte des Jôhannàn Bar Penkàjē," in *Nubia et Oriens Christianus: Festschrift für C.D.G. Müller,* edited by P.O. Scholz and R. Stempel (Cologne: Jürgen Dinter, 1987), 59–71; William G. Young, *Patriarch, Shah and Caliph: A Study of the Relationships of the Church of the East with the Sassanid Empire and the Early*

Caliphates up to 820 AD (Rawalpindi: Christian Study Centre, 1974), 99–105.

APOCALYPSE OF PSEUDO-METHODIUS

The secondary literature on the *Apocalypse of Pseudo-Methodius* is quite extensive. For a comprehensive bibliography of secondary literature up to 1993, see *CSCO* 541: xlviii–lxi. For a more select bibliography up to 2007, see *Christian-Muslim Relations,* 167–71. Due to space considerations, the following is much shorter than either of these. Nevertheless, it includes some of the most influential secondary literature on Pseudo-Methodius, as well as works published after 2007.

Glen W. Bowersock, "Helena's Bridle, Ethiopian Christianity, and Syriac Apocalyptic," *Studia Patristica* 45 (2010): 211–20; *Christian-Muslim Relations,* 163–70; *CSCO* 540 [edition]; *CSCO* 541 [German translation]; E. J. van Donzel, Andrea B. Schmidt, and Claudia Ott, *Gog and Magog in Early Eastern Christian and Islamic Sources: Sallam's Quest for Alexander's Wall* (Leiden: Brill, 2010), 26–32; Hoyland, *Seeing Islam,* 263–67; Francisco Javier Martinez, "Eastern Christian Apocalyptic in the Early Muslim Period: Pseudo-Methodius and Pseudo-Athanasius" (PhD dissertation, Catholic University of America, 1985) [English translation]; Palmer, *West-Syrian Chronicles,* 222–42 [English translation]; Gerrit J. Reinink, "Ismaël, der Wildesel in der Wüste: Zur Typologie der Apokalypse des Pseudo-Methodios," *Byzantinische Zeitschrift* 75 (1982): 336–44; Reinink, "Neue Erkenntnisse zur syrischen Textgeschichte des 'Pseudo-Methodius,'" in *Polyphonia Byzantina: Studies in Honour of Willem J. Aerts,* edited by Hero Hokwerda, Edmé R. Smits, and Marinus M. Woesthuis (Groningen: Egbert Fortsten, 1993), 85–96; Reinink, "Pseudo-Methodius und die Legende vom römischen Endkaiser," in *The Use and Abuse of Eschatology in the Middle Ages,* edited by W. Verbeke, D. Verhelst, and A. Welkenhuysen (Leuven: Leuven University Press, 1988), 82–111; Reinink, "Ps.-Methodius: A Concept of History in Response to the Rise of Islam," in *The Byzantine and Early Islamic East,* edited by Averil Cameron and Lawrence I. Conrad (Princeton: Darwin Press, 1992), 149–87; Reinink, "The Romance of Julian the Apostate as a Source for Seventh Century Syriac Apocalypses," in *La Syrie* de Byzance a l'Islam, VII*–VIII* Siècles, edited by Pierre Canivet and Jean-Paul Rey-Coquais (Damascus: Institut Français de Damas, 1992), 75–86; Reinink, Die Syrische Apokalypse des Pseudo-Methodius (Leuven: Peeters, 1993), 85–96; Reinink, "Tyrannen und Muslime: Die Gestaltung einer symbolischen Metapher bei Pseudo-Methodios," in Scripta Signa Vocis, edited by H.L.J. Vanstiphout, K. Jongeling, F. Leemhuis, and Reinink (Groningen: Egbert Forsten, 1986), 163–75; Stephen J. Shoemaker, "'The Reign of God Has Come': Eschatology and Empire in Late Antiquity and Early Islam," Arabica 61 (2014): 514–58; Suermann, Die geschichtstheologische Reaktion, 129–61 [edition and German translation]; Witold Witakowski, "The Eschatological Program of the Apocalypse of Pseudo-Methodios: Does It Make Sense?," Rocznik Orientalistyczny 53, no. 1 (2000): 33–42.

EDESSENE APOCALYPSE

Glen W. Bowersock, "Helena's Bridle, Ethiopian Christianity, and Syriac Apocalyptic," Studia Patristica 45 (2010): 211–20; Christian-Muslim Relations, 172–75; Hoyland, Seeing Islam, 267–68; Francisco Javier Martinez, "Eastern Christian Apocalyptic in the Early Muslim Period: Pseudo-Methodius and Pseudo-Athanasius" (PhD dissertation, Catholic University of America, 1985), 222–28 [edition and English translation]; François Nau, "Notices des manuscrits syriaque, éthiopiens et mandéens, entrés à la Bibliothèque Nationale de Paris depuis l'édition des catalogues," Revue de l'Orient Chretien 16 (1911): 302–5; Nau, "Révélations et légendes: Méthodius-Clément-Andronicus," Journal Asiatique 9 (1917): 425–34 [edition and French translation]; Palmer, West-Syrian Chronicles, 244–50 [English translation]; Gerrit J. Reinink, "Early Christian Reactions to the Building of the Dome of the Rock in Jerusalem," Xristianskij Vostok 2 (2002): 237–39; Reinink, "Der edessenische 'Pseudo-Methodius,'" Byzantinische Zeitschrift 83 (1990): 31–45; Suermann, Die geschichtstheologische Reaktion, 87–97 [edition], 162–74 [German translation]; William Wright, A Catalogue of the Syriac Manuscripts Preserved in the Library of the University of Cambridge (Cambridge: Cambridge University Press, 1901), 1194–97.

EXEGESIS OF THE PERICOPES OF
THE GOSPEL, ḤNANISHOʻ I

Hoyland, *Seeing Islam,* 200–203; Gerrit J. Reinink, "Fragmente der Evangelienexegese des Katholikos Henanišo I," in *V Symposium Syriacum, 1988,* edited by René Lavenant (Rome: Pontificium Institutum Studiorum Orientalium, 1990), 89–90.

LIFE OF THEODUṬĒ

EDSH, 408–9; Hoyland, *Seeing Islam,* 156–60; Andrew Palmer, "Āmīd in the Seventh-Century Syriac Life of Theodūṭē," in *The Encounter of Eastern Christianity with Early Islam,* edited by Emmanouela Grypeou, Mark N. Swanson, and David Thomas (Leiden: Brill, 2006), 111–38; Palmer, *Monk and Mason on the Tigris Frontier: The Early History of Tur 'Abdin* (Cambridge: Cambridge University Press, 1990), 88–91; Palmer, "Saints' Lives with a Difference: Elijah on John of Tella (d. 538) and Joseph on Theodotus of Amida (d. 698)," in *IV Symposium Syriacum, 1984,* edited by H.J.W. Drijvers, R. Lavenant, C. Molenberg, and G.J. Reinink (Rome: Pontificium Institutum Studiorum Orientalium, 1987), 203–16; Jack Tannous, "L'Hagiography syro-occidentale à la période Islamique," in *L'Hagiographie syriaque,* edited by André Binggeli, (Paris: Geuthner, 2012), 236–41; Tannous, "Syria between Byzantium and Islam: Making Incommensurables Speak" (PhD dissertation, Princeton University, 2010), 456–71.

COLOPHON OF *BRITISH LIBRARY*
ADDITIONAL 14,448

Sebastian Brock, "The Use of Hijra Dating in Syriac Manuscripts: A Preliminary Investigation," in *Redefining Christian Identity: Cultural Interaction in the Middle East since the Rise of Islam,* edited by J.J. van Ginkel, H.L. Murre-van den Berg, and T.M. van Lint (Leuven: Peeters, 2005), 278, 283; Wright, *Catalogue* 1:42–43.

APOCALYPSE OF JOHN THE LITTLE

Christian-Muslim Relations, 222–25; Han J.W. Drijvers, "Christians, Jews and Muslims in Northern Mesopotamia in Early Islamic Times: The Gospel of the Twelve Apostles and Related Texts," in *La Syrie de Byzance à l'Islam, VII*ᵉ*–VIII*ᵉ *Siècles*, edited by Pierre Canivet and Jean-Paul Rey-Coquais (Damascus: Institut Français de Damas, 1992), 67–74; Drijvers, "The Gospel of the Twelve Apostles: A Syriac Apocalypse from the Early Islamic Period," in *The Byzantine and Early Islamic East*, vol. 1, edited by Averil Cameron and Lawrence I. Conrad (Princeton: Darwin Press, 1991), 189–213; *EDSH*, 179; Mosche H. Goshen-Gottstein, *Syriac Manuscripts in the Harvard College Library: A Catalogue* (Missoula, MT: Scholars Press, 1979), 71; J. Rendel Harris, *The Gospel of the Twelve Apostles Together with the Apocalypses of Each One of Them* (Cambridge: Cambridge University Press, 1900) [edition and English translation]; Hoyland, *Seeing Islam*, 267–70; G.J. Reinink, "From Apocalyptics to Apologetics: Early Syriac Reactions to Islam," in *Endzeiten: Eschatologie in den monotheistischen Weltreligionen*, edited by Wolfram Brandes and Felicitas Schmieder (Berlin: Walter de Gruyter, 2008), 75–80; Suermann, *Die geschichtstheologische Reaktion*, 98–109 [edition], 175–91 [German translation].

CHRONICLE AD 705

Hoyland, *Seeing Islam*, 394–95; J.P.N. Land, *Anecdota Syriaca* (Leiden: E.J. Brill, 1862), 11 [edition and Latin translation]; François Nau, "Un colloque du patriarche Jean avec l'émir des Agaréens et faits divers des années 712 à 716," *Journal Asiatique* 11, no. 5 (1915): 226; Palmer, *West-Syrian Chronicles*, 43–44 [English translation]; Wright, *Catalogue* 2:992–93.

LETTERS, JACOB OF EDESSA

For a more complete bibliography, see Dirk Kruisheer, "A Bibliographical Clavis to the Works of Jacob of Edessa (Revised and Expanded)," in *Jacob of Edessa and the Syriac Culture of His Day*, edited by

Bas ter Haar Romeny (Leiden: Brill, 2008), 265–94. Some of the most important editions and studies include *Christian-Muslim Relations,* 226–33; *CSCO* 368 [edition]; *CSCO* 375 [English translation]; *EDSH,* 432–33; Jan J. van Ginkel, "Greetings to a Virtuous Man: The Correspondence of Jacob of Edessa," in Ter Haar Romeny, *Jacob of Edessa and the Syriac Culture of His Day,* 67–82; Van Ginkel, "History and Community: Jacob of Edessa and West Syrian Identity," in *Redefining Christian Identity: Cultural Interaction in the Middle East since the Rise of Islam,* edited by Van Ginkel, H.L. Murre-van den Berg, and T.M. van Lint (Leuven: Peeters, 2005), 67–76; Robert Hoyland, "Jacob and Early Islamic Edessa," in Ter Haar Romeny, *Jacob of Edessa and the Syriac Culture of His Day,* 11–24; Hoyland, "Jacob of Edessa on Islam," in *After Bardaisan: Studies on Continuity and Change in Syriac Christianity in Honour of Professor Han J.W. Drijvers,* edited by G.J. Reinink and A.C. Klugkist (Leuven: Peeters, 1999), 149–60; Hoyland, *Seeing Islam,* 160–67, 601–10; Gharighuriyus Yuhanna Ibrahim and George Anton Kiraz, eds., *Studies on Jacob of Edessa* (Piscataway, NJ: Gorgias Press, 2010); Konrad D. Jenner, "The Canons of Jacob of Edessa in the Perspective of the Christian Identity of His Day," in Ter Haar Romeny, *Jacob of Edessa and the Syriac Culture of His Day,* 101–12; C. Kayser, *Die Canones Jacobs von Edessa übersetzt und erläutert* (Leipzig: J.C. Hinrichs, 1886), 11–33 [edition and German translation]; Thomas J. Lamy, *Dissertatio de Syrorum fide et disciplina in re eucharista* (Leuven: Vanlinthout, 1859) [edition]; François Nau, *Les canons et les résolutions canoniques de Rabboula, Jean de Tella, Cyriaque d'Amid, Jacques d'Edesse, Georges des Arabes, Cyriaque d'Antioche, Jean III, Théodose d'Antioche et des Perses* (Paris: Lethielleux, 1906), 31–75 [edition and French translation]; Nau, "Lettre de Jacques d'Édesse sur la généalogie de la sainte vierge," *Revue de l'Orient Chrétien* 6 (1901): 512–31 [edition and French translation]; Karl-Erik Rignell, *A Letter from Jacob of Edessa to John the Stylite of Litarab Concerning Ecclesiastical Canons* (Lund: CWK Gleerup, 1979) [edition and English translation]; Alison Salvesen, "Jacob of Edessa's Life and Work: A Biographical Sketch," in Ter Haar Romeny, *Jacob of Edessa and the Syriac Culture of His Day,* 1–10; Uriel I. Simonsohn, "'Halting between Two Opinions': Conversion and Apostasy in Early Islam," *Medieval Encounters* 19 (2013): 362–64;

Herman G. B. Teule, "Jacob of Edessa and Canon Law," in Ter Haar Romeny, *Jacob of Edessa and the Syriac Culture of His Day*, 83–100.

CHRONICLE, JACOB OF EDESSA

E. W. Brooks, "The Chronological Canon of James of Edessa," *Zeitschrift der Deutschen Morgenländischen Gesellschaft* 53 (1899): 261–327; ibid., 54 (1900): 100–102; *Christian-Muslim Relations*, 231–32; *CSCO 5*: 261–330 [edition]; *CSCO 6*: 199–255 [Latin translation]; Amir Harrak, "Jacob of Edessa as a Chronicler," in *Studies on Jacob of Edessa*, edited by Gregorios Yohanna Ibrahim and George Anton Kiraz (Piscataway, NJ: Gorgias Press, 2010), 43–64; Hoyland, *Seeing Islam*, 165; Palmer, *West-Syrian Chronicles*, 36–40 [English translation]; Stephen J. Shoemaker, *The Death of a Prophet: The End of Muhammad's Life and the Beginnings of Islam* (Philadelphia: University of Pennsylvania Press, 2012), 36–38; Witold Witakowski, "The Chronicle of Jacob of Edessa," in *Jacob of Edessa and the Syriac Culture of His Day*, edited by Bas ter Haar Romeny (Leiden: Brill, 2008), 25–48; Wright, *Catalogue* 3:1062–64.

SCHOLIA, JACOB OF EDESSA

Bas ter Haar Romeny, "Jacob of Edessa on Genesis: His Quotations of the Peshitta and His Revision of the Text," in *Jacob of Edessa and the Syriac Culture of His Day*, edited by Haar Romeny (Leiden: Brill, 2008), 151–55; Dirk Kruisheer, "Reconstructing Jacob of Edessa's *Scholia*," in *The Book of Genesis in Jewish and Oriental Christian Interpretation: A Collection of Essays*, edited by Judish Frishman and Lucas Van Rompay (Leuven: Peeters, 1997), 187–96; George Phillips, *Scholia on Passages of the Old Testament* (London: Williams and Norgate, 1864), *25–*27, 39–42 [Edition and English translation]; Wright, *Catalogue* 2:591.

AGAINST THE ARMENIANS, JACOB OF EDESSA

Christian-Muslim Relations, 232–33; C. Kayser, *Die Canones Jacobs von Edessa übersetzt und erläutert* (Leipzig: J. C. Hinrichs, 1886), 4, 34–35 [edition and German translation].

KĀMED INSCRIPTIONS

Y. Elitzur and Zeʾev Erlich, "A New *bltmya* Inscription from Kāmed El-Lawz in the Lebanon Valley," *Journal of the American Oriental Society* 105 (1985): 711–14; P. Mouterde, "Inscriptions en syriaque dialectal à Kamed (Beqʿa)," *Mélanges de l'Université Saint-Joseph* 22 (1939): 77–106 [edition and French translation].

CHRONICLE OF DISASTERS

François Nau, "Un colloque du patriarche Jean avec l'émir des Agaréens et faits divers des années 712 à 716," *Journal Asiatique* 11, no. 5 (1915): 253–56 [edition and French translation]; Palmer, *West-Syrian Chronicles,* 45–48 [English translation]; Michael Philip Penn, "Monks, Manuscripts, and Muslims: Syriac Textual Changes in Reaction to the Rise of Islam," *Hugoye: Journal of Syriac Studies* 12, no. 2 (2009): 248–49; Wright, *Catalogue* 2:989–1003.

CHRONICLE AD 724

CSCO 5: 155 [edition]; *CSCO 6*: 119 [Latin translation]; Hoyland, *Seeing Islam,* 395–96; J.P.N. Land, *Anecdota Syriaca* (Leiden: E.J. Brill, 1862), 40 [edition and Latin translation]; Palmer, *West-Syrian Chronicles,* 49–50 [English translation]; Michael Philip Penn, "Monks, Manuscripts, and Muslims: Syriac Textual Changes in Reaction to the Rise of Islam," *Hugoye: Journal of Syriac Studies* 12, no. 2 (2009): 240–44; Penn, "Moving beyond the Palimpsest: Erasure in Syriac Manuscripts," *Journal of Early Christian Studies* 18, no. 2 (2010): 289–92; Wright, *Catalogue* 2:992–93.

DISPUTATION OF JOHN AND THE EMIR

David Bertaina, *Christian and Muslim Dialogues: The Religious Uses of a Literary Form in the Early Islamic Middle East* (Piscataway, NJ: Gorgias Press, 2011), 87–93; *Christian-Muslim Relations,* 782–85; Sidney H. Griffith, "Disputes with Muslims in Syriac Christian Texts: From Patriarch John (d.

648) to Bar Hebraeus (d. 1286)," in *Religionsgespräche im Mittelalter,* Wolfenbütteler Mittelalter-Studien 4, edited by Bernard Lewis and Friedrich Niewöhner (Wiesbaden: Otto Harrassowitz, 1992), 257–59; Hoyland, *Seeing Islam,* 459–65; François Nau, "Un colloque du patriarche Jean avec l'émir des Agaréens et faits divers des années 712 à 716," *Journal Asiatique* 11, no. 5 (1915): 225–47 [edition and French translation]; Michael Philip Penn, "John and the Emir: A New Introduction, Edition and Translation," *Le Muséon* 121 (2008): 83–109 [edition and English translation]; Gerrit J. Reinink, "The Beginnings of Syriac Apologetic Literature in Response to Islam," *Oriens Christianus* 77 (1993): 171–87; Barbara Roggema, "The Debate between Patriarch John and an Emir of the Mhaggrāyē: A Reconsideration of the Earliest Christian-Muslim Debate," in *Christians and Muslims in Dialogue in the Islamic Orient of the Middle Ages,* edited by Martin Tamcke (Beirut: Ergon Verlag, 2007), 21–39; Abdul Massih Saadi, "The Letter of John of Sedreh: A New Perspective on Nascent Islam," *Journal of the Assyrian Academic Society* 11, no. 1 (1997): 74–80, reprinted in *Journal of the Assyrian Academic Society* 1, no. 2 (1999): 54–64; Khalil Samir, "Qui est l'interlocuteur musulman du patriarche Syrien Jean III (631–648)?," in *IV Symposium Syriacum, 1984,* edited by H. J. W. Drijvers, R. Lavenant, C. Molenberg, and Reinink (Rome: Pontificium Institutum Studiorum Orientalium, 1987), 387–400; Harald Suermann, "The Old Testament and the Jews in the Dialogue between the Jacobite Patriarch John I and 'Umayr ibn Sa'd Al-Anṣārī," in *Eastern Crossroads: Essays on Medieval Christian Legacy,* edited by Juan Pedro Monferrer-Sala (Piscataway, NJ: Gorgias Press, 2007), 131–41; Suermann, "Orientalische Christen und der Islam: Christliche Texte aus der Zeit von 632–750," *Zeitschrift für Missionwissenschaft und Religionswissenschaft* 67 (1983): 125–28.

EXEGETICAL HOMILIES, MĀR ABBĀ II

Gerrit J. Reinink, "An Early Syriac Reference to Qur'an 112?," in *All Those Nations ... Cultural Encounters within and with the Near East,* edited by H. L. J. Vanstiphout (Groningen: Styx Publications, 1999), 123–30; Reinink, "Political Power and Right Religion in the East Syrian Disputation between a Monk of Bēt Ḥālē and an Arab Notable," in *The*

Encounter of Eastern Christianity with Early Islam, edited by Emmanouela Grypeou, Mark N. Swanson, and David Thomas (Leiden: Brill, 2006), 155–57; Reinink, "Die Textüberlieferung der Gannat Bussame," *Le Muséon* 90 (1977): 111–15.

DISPUTATION OF BĒT ḤALĒ

David Bertaina, *Christian and Muslim Dialogues: The Religious Uses of a Literary Form in the Early Islamic Middle East* (Piscataway, NJ: Gorgias Press, 2011), 138–45; *Christian-Muslim Relations,* 268–73; Sidney H. Griffith, "Christians, Muslims and the Image of the One God: Iconophilia and Iconophobia in the World of Islam in Umayyad and Early Abbasid Times," in *Die Welt der Götterbilder,* edited by Brigitte Groneberg and Hermann Spieckermann (New York: Walter de Gruyter, 2007), 347–80; Griffith, "Disputing with Islam in Syriac: The Case of the Monk of Bēt Ḥālē and a Muslim Emir," *Hugoye: Journal of Syriac Studies* 3 (2000): 29–54; Griffith, *Syriac Writers on Muslims and the Religious Challenge of Islam* (Kottayam, Kerala: St. Ephrem Ecumenical Research Institute, 1995), 26–37; Hoyland, *Seeing Islam,* 465–572; Peter Jager, "Intended Edition of a Disputation between a Monk of the Monastery of Bet Hale and One of the Ṭayoye," *IV Symposium Syriacum, 1984,* edited by H.J.W. Drijvers, R. Lavenant, C. Molenberg, and G.J. Reinink (Rome: Pontificium Institutum Studiorum Orientalium, 1987), 401–2; Reinink, "Bible and Qur'an in Early Syriac Christian-Islamic Disputation," in *Christians and Muslims in Dialogue in the Islamic Orient of the Middle Ages,* edited by Martin Tamcke (Beirut: Ergon Verlag, 2007), 57–72; Reinink, "Following the Doctrine of the Demons: Early Christian Fear of Conversion to Islam," in *Cultures of Conversions,* edited by Jan N. Bremmer, Wout J. van Bekkum, and Arie L. Molendijk (Leuven: Peeters, 2006), 134–37; Reinink, "From Apocalyptics to Apologetics: Early Syriac Reactions to Islam," in *Endzeiten: Eschatologie in den monotheistischen Weltreligionen,* edited by Wolfram Brandes and Felicitas Schmieder (Berlin: Walter de Gruyter, 2008), 82–87; Reinink, "The Lamb on the Tree: Syriac Exegesis and Anti-Islamic Apologetics," in *The Sacrifice of Isaac: The Aqedah (Genesis 22) and Its Interpretations,* edited by Ed Noort and Eibert Tigchelaar (Leiden: Brill, 2002), 109–24; Reinink, "Political

Power and Right Religion in the East Syrian Disputation between a Monk of Bēt Ḥalē and an Arab Notable," in *The Encounter of Eastern Christianity with Early Islam,* edited by Emmanouela Grypeou, Mark N. Swanson, and David Thomas (Leiden: Brill, 2006), 153–70; Reinink, "The Veneration of Icons, the Cross, and the Bones of the Martyrs in an Early East-Syrian Apology against Islam," in *Bibel, Byzanz und Christlicher Orient: Festschrift für Stephen Gerö zum 65. Geburtstag,* edited by D. Bumazhnov, E. Grypeou, T.B. Sailors, and A. Toepel (Leuven: Peeters, 2011), 329–42; Addai Scher, "Notice sur les manuscrits syriaques et arabes conservés à l'archevêché chaldéen de Diarbékir," *Journal Asiatique* 10 (1907): 395–98; David Taylor, forthcoming in *Christsein in der islamischen Welt,* Sven Grebenstein and Sidney Griffith, eds. [English translation].

INDEX